THE SMART SALES METHOD

2017
UPDATE

JOE MORONE

KAREN BENJAMIN

MARTY SMITH

Dedication

This book is dedicated to all B2B technology CEO's and company leaders.

Through your innovation, intelligence and courage, the world becomes a more prosperous and safer place for us to live.

May you all be successful in all that you do.

Acknowledgements

This book would not have been possible without the examples, insight and, above all, the extensive research of literally generations of expert sales persons, students of sales, and sales analysts.

We particularly wish to thank Neil Rackham, author of *Spin Selling*; Matthew Dixon and Brent Adamson, lead authors of *The Challenger Sale* and *The Challenger Customer*; Robert B. Miller and Stephen E. Heiman, lead authors of *Strategic Selling* and *The New Conceptual Selling*; and, of course, the "Greatest Generation" – Zig Ziglar and Dale Carnegie.

We also particularly wish to express our thanks for the ongoing efforts of our colleagues, the Objective Management Group, whose detailed studies of over 700,000 sales personnel have been instrumental in the development of modern sales approaches, and of our own sales methodology.

To the Worldteam members, we learn from your examples every day. Thank you.

Table of Contents

FOREWORD

Commitment to Fact-Based Consulting

The Smart Sales Methodology is a statistically supported approach, specifically tailored to maximize business-to-business technology sales results.

No sales training or sales methodology in B2B technology sales has been more empirically grounded, more tested in practice, or shown to be more effective.

The roots of the Smart Sales Method stem from the ground-breaking research conducted by the Huthwaite Corporation, whose 12-year multi-million-dollar study of 35,000 sales calls has been called, "the best documented account of sales success ever collected."

The second source is the survey of over 6,000 sales reps across the globe and across industries done by the Forbes 100 member-based advisory group that appeared in the New York Times Challenger Sale series of best sellers.

The third source is the continuous findings of the Objective Management Group (OMG), a sales person and sales candidate testing and evaluation company that has compiled the world's largest database of information on sales practices, based on assessments of nearly 750,000 salespeople over the past 24 years.

The Smart Sales Method was developed during a recorded 25-year span of progressive growth in B2B technology sales by its principal developers Joe Morone, Karen Benjamin and Marty Smith of Worldleaders Inc.

There is no sales methodology in B2B technology sales whose elements are more grounded in hard data, more extensively tested and researched, or proven more effective.

CHAPTER ONE

NOTHING HAPPENS UNTIL SOMETHING IS SOLD

Chapter One

When you're the CEO or Leader, all the people around you are depending on you. They're your colleagues, your friends and your family. Their ability to feed their families, educate their children and cover their bills depends on you. And all of that hangs on one thing: Sales.

Sales is revenue.

Sales is cash flow.

Sales enables research and development. Sales covers payroll. Sales drives profit.

Sales is survival.

We understand that, for you, *nothing happens until something is sold.* This is your life.

As a business leader you're comfortable dealing with the hard facts, making analytical decisions and handling challenging situations. That's why you're in the leadership role.

When you're in front of the right customer, under the right circumstances, you get the job done. You can sell. You understand how your offerings impact your customer's business performance. You're able to negotiate a price that both sides can live with. And many times you can get a transaction back on track within a conversation or two. That's why you're in the leadership role!

You may have superstars on your team that can do it too. So why can't the rest of the sales team sell effectively? You've tried it all. You've hired them all. It's just not happening. When you ask questions everything seems to be so fuzzy, unclear and uncertain. Why do you keep hearing the same things over and over again?

"People buy from who they like."

"Our price is too high, quality too low, there's no differentiation."

"We have a long sales cycle."

Is it all true? Are you simply too impatient? Are your products or services out of line with the competition? Do you have a 'me-too' product?

May I ask you three simple questions to see if we can discover the answers together?

1. *Likability.* When you're involved in buying decisions for your *own* organization, would you buy from a sales team that had the ability to teach you how to improve your business competitiveness, reduce

operational costs, and better achieve compliance? Or would you ignore all that and buy from the most likable person that called on you?

If you answered that you'd buy from the most likable person, please close this book and throw it away right now. (OK, I'm having a little fun here. Just because this book is statistically driven, it doesn't mean we can't have a little fun reading it!) Of *course* you're going to buy from the thought leader. This is statistically supported.

2. *Price vs. Quality.* How many products or services did you buy last year that you can validate represent the highest quality in the marketplace? Conversely, how many products or services did you buy last year that you were able to validate represented the absolute lowest price in the marketplace?

The majority of sophisticated buyers decide on the *best fit* to their organization's needs at the time that they're making the purchasing decision. Not the best, not the lowest. The best fit overall.

We call this Relative Value. In the Smart Sales Method, relative value is represented by the formula RV=Business Return (BR) + Risk Mitigation (RM), sold at Fair Market Price (FMP). More on **RV=BR+RM@FMP** in a moment.

3. *Six, Twelve, Eighteen Month Sales Cycles.* Do you or your leadership team regularly begin evaluating B2B purchases for your organization six, twelve, eighteen months before you're going to make

the decision?

When B2B and many B2G buyers were asked the question, "Why are you waiting six, twelve, eighteen months before making a purchasing decision?" what do you think the answer was? The majority of the responses were (and are) that they intend to buy now or within the quarter, but the sales cycle drags out. The primary reason? Because the internal stakeholders were unclear on how to come to a conclusion. (More on this in following chapters.)

The point here is that top B2B sales teams are able to (1) teach their customers how to improve a business result, (2) lead their customer through an objective evaluation process, and (3) close the sale using the Relative Value equation:

$$RV = BR + RM@FMP$$

When done effectively, sales closure rates move from the estimated 3%-10% to a healthy 70% or more.

This is Smart Selling.

The rest of this book is dedicated to providing you with guidance to implement 3 simple steps, performed in a linear format. This is The Smart Sales Method for B2B technology sales teams.

Decades of independent research plus our own study of the top 6% of successful sales performers

TEACH

TEACH CLIENTS HOW TO IMPROVE A *BUSINESS RESULT*

1. IMPROVE SALES, REV MARKET PENETRATION
2. REDUCE CYCLE/WORK TIME
3. IMPROVE FIRST TIME QUALITY
4. MEET LEGAL/POLITICAL COMPLIANCE
5. IMPROVE PROFIT/SAVE MONEY

LEAD

LEAD ALL STAKEHOLDERS THROUGH A CONCLUSIVE EVALUATION PROCESS

- BUSINESS LEVEL DECISION MAKER
- USER LEVEL DECISION MAKER
- PROCUREMENT DECISION MAKER

CLOSE

CLOSE ON THE TRANSACTION GO/NO BASED ON RELATIVE VALUE

$$RV = BR + RM @ FMP$$

have allowed us to build a new and very different picture of what best practices mean in a complex B2B technology-selling environment.

Credible, objective, third party research has been done on literally hundreds of thousands of sales practices relevant to your business. That research has allowed us to build an extraordinarily effective way of building a clear, clean, lean and dependable sales methodology.

This book is a blueprint of that method. It's short, tight, and to the point. It'll walk you through the Smart Sales Method in less than an hour. Read it and you'll learn exactly what you need to do to push your sales force up into the ranks of the top sales performers, and raise your sales and your company to the ranks of the market leaders.

But there's one thing it won't do.

It won't put it into effect for you.

That's your job.

Some executive leaders leave that to others. Many of them leave it to their sales department. Maybe you're thinking of doing this.

Maybe you've been avoiding the uncomfortable job of coming to grips with sales for years.

Please don't push it down. It won't get done the way it needs to be done. You're the one who's got to take charge of your sales process and your sales team. You're the one who's got to get personally involved and get a solid, practical, fact-driven methodology set up.

Because nothing happens until something is sold.

And nothing is sold until you put an effective sales team and sales methodology in place to sell it. We know enough already to have developed a methodology that has gotten results in the field that leave earlier approaches far behind. We present it here. We call it the Smart Sales Method.

Sit down, take an hour, and read through the rest of this book. We believe it will transform your understanding of sales — and your business.

Make it work. And make your business the success it was meant to be.

If you need help, just call, text or email me.

Joe Morone
www.worldleaderssales.com
LinkedIn.com/in/increasesales
Email: jmorone@worldleaderssales.com
Mobile or text: (585) 732-5666

WHAT USED TO WORK DOESN'T WORK ANYMORE

Chapter Two

In the past few years the traditional ways of selling have become less and less effective.

Don't take our word for it. The world's acknowledged leader in providing reliable B2B sales performance data is the Objective Management Group. Citing Objective Management Group statistics, CEO David Kurlan says, "74% of all sales people have less than 20% of the skills required to sell competitively in today's B2B marketplace."

Studies show that only 26% of sales people today are finding new business consistently, and closing the kinds of deals critical to your business' survival.

The rest of them aren't.

But they *are* on the phone. They *are* meeting with customers. They're taking the traditional approaches. And they're doing it in the classic ways. They have strong product knowledge, they're willing to be flexible on price, and they're very likable, and very service-oriented.

And that's the problem. The old ways no longer work.

What's changed in the past few years? Why aren't the traditional approaches working?

In the B2B selling environment there are four major changes occurring:

• Buyers No Longer Need to Talk To Salespeople For Product Or Services Information

The Internet has created a global marketplace for buyers, and this has enabled a tremendous amount of comparison-shopping.

At any time, from any place, from the head office on down, your customers can pull out their smartphone, go online, reach across geographic borders, and access not just your product or service information, not just user reviews, not just product ratings, not just your company track record, not just your personal information and business rumors, but all of your competitor's information too, and all at the press of a button.

• More Decision-Makers From More Business Units

Buying decisions today require higher levels of sign-off and involve more and more decision makers. The challenge is in gaining consensus from not one but an ever-growing number of decision makers who often have competing perspectives, requirements and agendas. Gaining access and developing credibility and buy-in with all of the right decision-makers – even identifying them – is one of the most significant barriers in corporate sales today.

• Difficulty Creating Differentiation Between The Top 3 To 5 Competitors

With the abundance of easily accessible information, competing providers are now able to gain far more competitive intelligence on each other's offerings, and match or duplicate them far more quickly and easily. This results in more parity across the field.

• Intensified Scrutiny And Purchasing Control

The combination of increasing product parity and economic recession means that corporations are engaging in competitive bidding far more often and in far more types of purchases than ever before. The number of RFP's, and now of reverse auctions, are exploding – and the rate of profitability per sale is declining.

And how are sales reps responding to these changes? Mostly by doing more of the same things they did in the nineteenth century. Relying on charisma. Making call after call. Setting up product demonstrations and doing the things that used to work when B2B buying and selling was much less sophisticated.

Despite the fact that analysis shows that today those ways are no longer working.

Take "building relationships." That's the cornerstone of the previous top sales approach — still the most popular, most recommended, default sales approach among many sales managers.

But what do the studies that track actual performance results say?

Barely 4% of the top sales reps are managing to make the "relationship" approach work anymore.

Why?

Because the real decision makers in a B2B sale are more concerned with knowing how your product or service will (a) improve their sales or market penetration, (b) reduce their operational cycle time, (c) improve first-time quality, (d) enhance compliance, or (e) improve profitability and/or cost reduction.

Sales reps still using outdated approaches will tell you that people buy from sales people they like.

While the stats say people buy from sales reps that can best help them improve their *competitive position.*

Another example of what's changed? Let's look at the tremendous amount of confusion over how to best contact a new prospect. Personal visit? Telephone? Email? Inmail? Text? Skype? Facebook, Twitter, Instagram, Pinterest, IM chat?

There's so much sheer choice out there now that many reps are just jumping from one new thing to the next, and not using any of them effectively.

Another factor is how and when the purchasing or procurement organization is involved. The emphasis on costs stemming from a slow economy has given procurement more visibility than ever before. Yet, in most instances the cost, risk and business value requirements are not fully understood by the purchasing professional involved.

The untrained salesperson will simply shrug their shoulders and say, "The lowest price always gets it" – even when the actual stats show that, when the real requirements are fully understood, price is only 9% of a B2B buying decision.

Last, but perhaps most important, we discovered a simple barrier that almost all sales managers and B2B sales training organizations have overlooked.

Contrary to what sales people are told by the customer, most organizations that you're selling to today have no consistent approach for evaluating and buying innovative new technologies. Sure, they know how to buy consumables, replacements and upgrades, but have no consistent approach for evaluating new ideas.

Because so many organizations are involving so

many different stakeholders from different business units, it's seldom that a clear acceptance criterion is set, measured and decided on, in a timely fashion.

The top 6% technology sales people know how to teach a client a new way of improving their competitiveness, how to lead them through their evaluation process and how to close the sale on relative value.

This is a new skill that requires training, practice and guidance.

And you, the CEO, need to lead *them*, by helping develop them into a sales force whose activities align with newer, smarter, statistically supported methods.

As we said in the opening sentence of this book, "When you're the CEO or Leader, all the people around you are depending on you." By implementing a sales methodology, you will take a big step forward in creating competitive advantage, independence and sustainability within your entire organization.

We have those new methods. We've studied them, simplified them, synthesized them, applied them and *won* with them.

Read on and you will too.

CHAPTER THREE

WHAT WORKS NOW AND WHY

Chapter Three

Close to three-quarters of a million studies have been done to distinguish effective sales approaches from poor ones.

As the hard data and insights grew, much of it reached the business public in the form of best-selling books and striking new sales concepts.

We evaluated those studies to see which approaches had the highest statistical probability of generating successful sales when applied specifically to B2B technology selling environments.

At worldleaderssales.com we reference some of the most valuable of those books and studies. They were key factors, along with our nearly thirty years of field experience, in helping us figure out what really works and what doesn't.

But pointing you to earlier studies, earlier stages, and abstract concepts won't tell you what you need to know to get your sales reps selling right *now*. You need the exact steps, and you need to see how they flow seamlessly into a repeatable sales methodology.

That's how the rest of this book is structured.

This chapter covers what works now – the way

buyers buy today. We cover the unique sequence and structure of sales methods that make up The Smart Sales Method, then we show how that method translates directly into a unique deal flow for selling B2B technology solutions.

The remainder of the book zeros in on applying the tools and skills needed to implement Smart Sales Methods directly with maximum impact.

Let's do it.

Why And How Buyers Buy

Many experts have competing opinions on why and how people and organizations buy.

Nearly all of them can be boiled down to three scenarios.

One is *logic*. Management consulting firms like McKinsey stress the need for organizations to buy rationally. So they provide heavy return-on-investment analysis. There's plenty of Six Sigma dialogue on cutting out waste. There's heavy emphasis on corporate decision-making skills. To this group, it's all about specs and numbers: buyers buy from the seller that makes the most tightly reasoned case.

The next expert opinion on how best to sell involves *emotion*. If you talk to the Emotional Quotient people or know the EQ belief system, they feel that all buying decisions are ultimately emotional buying decisions. Gut feeling comes first — fear, greed, irrational desire. Logic only comes in later – if ever. These experts claim buyers always buy from the heart and from the gut, and they find reasons to justify the purchase after the fact. The EQ case has plausible support. We've all bought things impulsively; we've all done things because we felt them to be right, without always having hard evidence demonstrating it to be right.

The third idea is *survival.* It's based on the Hierarchy of Needs pyramid developed by psychologist Dr. Abraham Maslow. Maslow's studies showed that while many different drivers motivate people, some are primal and fundamental. And the most fundamental is the survival instinct. According to Maslow, people buy to satisfy needs, and no need is more strong and basic and powerful than the naked need to survive, personally and professionally.

There's no question as to whether or not these theories work, or even which works. They all work. We all feel. We all reason. We all want to survive. The problem is, most sales people focus on only one of the three when they sell. While the truth is, at some level every buying decision involves all three. All three needs have to be addressed.

Sometimes, in actual practice, they are. But at different times some sales reps will favor one approach, some will favor another, some will glide from approach to approach, and none of these approaches will necessarily sync up with the person they're trying to sell to at the time. The problem is not that the approaches don't work, or that they're not used. The problem is that they're not used in the right *order*.

The real question is how best to *structure* them, so that the key drivers work together in the right *sequence*, powerfully and effectively, making the most decisive collective impact, and gaining the maximum yield.

Because normally sales reps apply them in the worst possible, *least* effective, ways.

Look at logic, emotion and survival in the standard sales literature. That's the order that you'll see — L, E, S. They give the buyer a logical reason (features, functions) to buy their product or service. They hope the buyer will get emotional and excited about it. Finally they hope the buyer will believe that they and their business just can't survive without it.

That is exactly backwards. Exactly wrong. *Perfectly* wrong.

Experience has shown us that *the strongest, primary driver behind a buying decision is the buyer's survival instinct.* Survival buyers are buyers who feel that they need this product or service to advance the competitive strength and prosperity of their company, and in that way to advance their personal and professional status in the company. And buyers who see such purchases in terms of their own business survival are in the majority: people care about their job and their job security first. They attach their survival to making the right buying choice and advancing the goals of the company. But their core driver is to secure or advance *themselves.*

The person can be a business leader, or a senior engineer or a procurement professional. They're each different, and in certain ways they need to be handled differently. But fundamentally they're driven by the same need – to survive in an often unforgiving corporate environment focused on performance success.

In most business-to-business sales, the survival instinct of the buyer is positional: the survival instinct drives that buyer's willingness and readiness to advance their career, and to do that by doing his or her job more effectively or by receiving recognition for driving profit and innovation.

So when we look at how to apply the survival component, we want to present what this deal means personally to each person in the company involved in the buying decision. That evokes *survival.*

When someone is in their survival mode, if the

sales rep were to ask two simple questions about the deal — "Why? Why now?" — this would cause a response ranging from fear, excitement, anger, vigilance. That evokes emotion.

If the same sales rep were then to suggest a logical next step like "Let's get together to determine feasibility, potential return and see if we're the right fit," that question at that time would best appeal to the customer's reason. That evokes *logic*.

The SEL Model

That's why we call it the *SEL* model — Survival, Emotion, Logic, in that order. Because it moves in the opposite sequence from the usual approach, and *starts* with survival. Emotion is the wrong entry point. If a buyer can be made to see that their survival in the corporate environment is involved, emotion – intense emotion, alert interest – automatically follows.

So when we talk to a customer about a business goal or a problem they face, when we can sense that it touches on their instinct for survival, when we see that it's put them in a survival mode, we simply focus on that. We ask them — "Why? Why is that important or interesting to you?" Simply asking them that will take it to a personal level and automatically trigger an emotional response. If we ask them, "Why is it important now?" what comes to their mind is either fear that they're going to lose an opportunity

SURVIVAL

HOW MANY BIDS DID YOU LOSE
IN THE PAST 12 MONTHS
BECAUSE YOU COULDN'T
MEET SPECIFICATIONS, TIMING, OR
BUDGET REQUIREMENTS?

EMOTION

IS IMPROVING
YOUR COMPETITIVENESS
IMPORTANT OR INTERESTING
TO YOU? WHY? WHY NOW?
WHAT ARE THE CONSEQUENCES
OF WAITING?

LOGIC

LET'S GET TOGETHER
IN ORDER TO DETERMINE
FEASIBILITY, POTENTIAL RETURN
AND TO SEE IF WE'RE
THE RIGHT FIT.

or take a loss, or anxiety that they may have to bear the blame, or excitement at the chance to shine in the company's eyes.

The questions "Why" and "Why now?" form part two of the SEL model: the emotional trigger. That's where people become personally, emotionally involved.

And from there we move straight into logic. We say, "Let's get together to determine whether making an improvement to your business is *feasible*, whether there's a potentially strong *return*, and whether or not we're the best *fit* to make it happen."

In other words, we move the conversation forward to see if our offering can be implemented so as to deliver a clear competitive advantage to the buyer's business, and to see if both our firms can work together effectively.

The SEL model allows the sales rep to align survival, emotion and logic in an order that best enables the customer or decision team to work out what's most important to their personal job survival and to their company's survival.

Once survival is evoked, the feelings it inspires drives the conversation to progress further until you the seller can satisfy that interest with a direct (logical) assessment determining feasibility, potential return, and best fit; that's what drives the whole sales cycle.

The SEL model is the perfect way to align all of

the most powerful buying drivers in a B2B sale into a simple and effective structure that will give anyone who applies it the highest probability of success in selling.

A New Era

How is this structured approach different from the usual, *un*-structured, *un*-successful approaches?

It's totally different.

We like to make a distinction between three eras in selling — Era 1, Era 2, and Era 3.

Era 1 in many ways came down to a simple brute force numbers approach. The sales rep would visit or cold call literally thousands of prospects in hope that some one of them would be interested in listening to their product or services description. Many sales reps still do.

Yet the data clearly indicates that this not only chews up a massive amount of time and resources, but that the vast majority of people contacted in that way don't respond or respond negatively. On top of that, sales reps experience so much rejection and failure with that approach that it drives tremendous, constant and costly turnover.

And what if, one of those times, a prospect does show interest, and agrees to sit through the sales person's pitch? Usually the rep talks product,

product, product, and does "not take no for an answer" — sometimes until forcibly ejected. That usually doesn't turn into a sale either.

What do they do next? They just follow with more of the same brute force approach: endless, useless, follow-up calls and emails.

Why did people do it that way? Why do some still do it? Because, if the final sale brings in enough of a profit to cover the time and costs involved in securing the sale, it's profitable. It works. Just not well. So not well that the costly waste and continual turnover involved in this unstructured, scatter-shot approach proved to be too much. By the Seventies, sales researchers began making major efforts to find a better way.

Era 2 selling resulted from those efforts. As the research grew, new and different and more effective ways of selling began to emerge. Most had certain core characteristics in common. You've probably heard of them. Solution selling was one of the new approaches. Consultative Selling was another. Customer-Centered Sales, Complex Sales and Relationship Selling were still others.

They all had a basic, sound, and positive advantage over Era 1. And that was that they focused on the buyer, not the seller. Sales reps began to ask questions, to study the company's needs, to learn about the buyer's wishes and to try to meet them. They began to customize their product or service and try to provide a unique solution to a unique business problem.

If product-centered repetition was at the heart of Era 1, "Ask good questions" was the heart of Era 2.

And since trying to actively find out what buyers wanted involved more knowledge-intensive, personal and creative selling approaches, it *did* serve to heighten and extend the skills of sales professionals. It *did* lead to more lucrative complex sales.

But it had drawbacks too. It could be as time-intensive and labor-intensive as Era 1. Crafting deeply customized complex solutions could be a major effort — and still might not sell or prove very profitable in the end.

And even when it did, the customized, extremely complex solution might just plain not work that well when actually implemented. Complicated solutions have more ways to go off the rails than simple ones.

The truth is, for all its emphasis on complexity, this approach was fundamentally as unstructured as the earlier one. The sales rep listened to the buyer, and followed wherever the buyer led. Sometimes that worked. And sometimes it led to disaster.

You see, the problem with Era 2 selling was that it involved asking the buyer what they wanted, and then just providing it, without considering whether it was what the buyer *needed* as opposed to wanted. Sometimes the buyers weren't sure what they wanted. Sometimes they wanted the wrong thing. The solutions they asked for were not always tied to a positive business result or a best-fit for their specific situation.

Finding those solutions eventually led to the new benchmark-driven Era 3 approach.

In Era 3 the sales person defines an ideal end state or cites a benchmark that enables the customer to realize a tangible competitive advantage within their marketplace. The objective is to teach the client how to get an improved business result — *not* to ask the customer what they think they need.

The difference between Era 2 and Era 3 is that the responsibility for defining that ideal end-state is on the *salesperson*, not the customer. In Era 1 and Era 2 the customer is always right. In Era 3 the *salesperson* has to be right — and to teach the customer a new and objectively better way to improve their business. The Smart Sales person is leading, not following.

The strength of the Smart Sales Method, and the reason it's the highest probability sales methodology, is that it applies the concepts of Era 3, delivered within the structured sequence of the SEL model. The Smart Sales Method goes for primal survival motivation first, flows seamlessly into emotion, then builds and presents a solidly logical and rational analysis built around the best way to advance a prospect's business and the prospect's position within that business.

So how does the SEL model work in terms of an actual deal? What are the steps?
Here's how.

Structuring The Smart Dealflow

The core drivers of the SEL model — survival, emotion, and logic — develop naturally and powerfully into three simple action steps. They're easily understood and easily sequenced.

We call them *Survey*, *Assess*, and *Align*.

Survey

What other sales professionals call Prospecting we call Surveying. In many ways it covers much the same ground.

When we conduct a Survey, we simply ask a client if they are aware of or interested in achieving a specific desirable business outcome, or have a need to improve their competitive position. When we survey a customer we're not *asking* them if they want to buy something — we're *stating* a potential competitive advantage for that customer, and we're asking that customer whether there's an interest or a need to achieve it. We're asking that customer if they're interested in improving a business result — in making more money, or saving more money, or meeting compliance. We simply and directly ask the customer if there's any interest in making their company stronger, better and more competitive in some objectively measurable way. If there is, that by itself will be sufficient to secure the first part of the

SEL — survival.

An example would be calling on a CEO and asking them if they feel that their sales team is winning big enough and often enough. If they are, there's nothing more to say. But if they want or need or are under pressure to do better – and they usually are – that alone will put the first part of the SEL model into effect. That alone will trigger the survival instinct.

Then we ask the next question: "Is that important or interesting to you? Why? Why now?"

That triggers an emotional response (vigilance, fear, disgust, anger) — the emotional second component of the SEL.

(Spotting it isn't something you'll need to wonder about. When that customer says, "*Of course* we're not winning big enough or often enough. *Yes,* we *need* to get better results, and we need to see them by the end of this quarter," you'll know you've touched a nerve.)

And if we then say, "OK, let's get together to determine potential feasibility, return on investment, and best fit," what we're saying is, let's get together and find out if what you want is possible, if it's worth doing, and if together we can make it happen.

After all, how can a business leader *not* want to know if an important and measurable improvement can be made, if it's clearly profitable, and if you can deliver it? That's taken us all the way through the process to logic; and that begins the sales cycle.

The 5x1

There's a tool we use to get through this Survey process smoothly and easily. We call that tool the 5x1 ("Five By One") because it quickly and easily allows a sales person to survey a customer for need or interest in the first five seconds, and, within one minute, to convert that interest into a qualified lead.

In the first five seconds, they're able to trigger the customer's survival instinct simply by asking a specific question that addresses their professional survival.

Here's one example of a 5x1 template opening:

"We work every day with executives or managers like you to improve_____ [*sales results, operational effectiveness, product or service quality, compliance and/or safety or profitability*] by providing_____ [*your solution or offerings*]."

Or it can be put as a simple but provocative question:

"Are you doing as well [*in a business-specific area*] as you'd like to be? Would you like to see improved results [*in that business-specific area*]?"

Unless there is *no* area in which they crave

better results – and in the business world that doesn't happen very often – the answer is yes.

That's when we add the second component. We ask, "*Is that important or interesting to you?*"

If they live and breathe and have a heartbeat, it almost certainly is.

"*Why? Why now?*"

That gets prospects themselves thinking about their motivational drivers, their needs, their goals, the time pressures they're facing. When that process starts to run, it's already triggering their emotions.

And when we then suggest a conversation to simply *assess* whether that's do-able and profitable, we're triggering that customer's logic.

The sales rep is able to get through the entire SEL concept using the 5x1 in literally one ("1") minute!

Why is this so effective? Because we're opening up a conversation by immediately talking to a customer about *their* competitive position, *their* competitive advantage, *their* advancement, and *not* about *us*, and *our* need to make a sale.

Most sales people feel a need to talk about how great their product is, how great their service is, how great their company is, how great *they* are, right out of the gate.

Buyers don't care! Not yet. Yes, ultimately they'll want to know your firm is qualified. But, initially, they care about *themselves* and about whether the seller can help *them*, and *how*. When you address *that*, they listen.

The most important thing about our sales methodology is that it's all about the *customer's* ability to better navigate their business situation, about the *customer's* need to grow market share and save on costs or build revenue, as opposed to our need to sell something to them.

Our focus is on teaching the customer how to better compete. So we directly address their competitiveness in the first five seconds of the 5x1.

That's the beauty of it. They're engaged because we're drawing out what most engages them: their job survival, their business survival, their emotional involvement in that survival, and we're addressing the clear, measurable, objective steps needed to make it happen.

Assess

By the end of the 5x1, we're already moving into the concluding component of the SEL model – logic. We're at the point of proposing and scheduling the Fit-Assessment.

What's a Fit-Assessment? That's what happens when the sales executive suggests a conversation with the customer and affected stakeholders in the company to determine if they can achieve an objective, measurable, profitable business improvement with the seller's help.

A discussion takes place to determine whether the competitive advantage raised during the 5x1 can be achieved, and if the seller's product or services can effectively and competitively help them achieve it. It may take place on-site; it may take place over a conference call. It could take a few days of investigation and analysis; it could take just a few questions.

What are we looking to assess? The potential business impact of our solution. Any potential risks or disruptions. Solutions previously considered. Technical feasibility. Constraints. Priorities. Budget justification. We have a specific set of questions (which we'll shortly be presenting in detail) that we ask during the assessment to both instill and distill information from the customer. Those questions enable us to put together a complete and accurate listing of the business and technical requirements we need to know in order to build a well-aligned proposal — what we call the Smart Proposal.

Going in, the assessment phase is a discussion aimed at determining if the seller has a feasible likelihood of enabling a customer to achieve a better competitive result.

Closing out the assessment phase, we've gained a complete and accurate set of business and technical requirements.

Once we have that, we enter stage three, the final stage: the Alignment phase.

Align

The Alignment phase focuses on a document that we'll examine in detail in an upcoming chapter: the Smart Proposal. In the Smart Proposal we're simply and briefly taking the business objectives and constraints that we captured from the customer in the course of the assessment, aligning it with our solution and our capabilities, and then describing that alignment and how well it serves the objectives of that customer's survival criteria. We're describing in plain and simple terms how our offer can enable that customer to win more sales, reduce operational cycle time, improve quality, meet compliance and earn more profit.

The Assessment phase shows whether our solution is viable. If it is, then, in the Alignment stage, we construct and present our Smart Proposal and simply run through how that solution is built.

The key to remember is that the Smart Proposal is a sequential way of keeping the customer focused on their business objectives. The order in which it's done follows those business objectives, and is simply a crystal clear statement and understanding of what the customer needs to do to be more competitive.

The first component specifically outlines the business objectives and their alignment to the survival of the organization. The second component is a short review of the alternative strategies that we've both considered. The third component is the solutions overview. The fourth is scope, schedule, and cost. The fifth describes the solution provider's unique or distinguishing qualifications. The last component is a short – very short – overview of your organization.

Again, our model is perfectly backwards from the other models. Other proposals start off with the company overview and talk about why they're so great. Our approach focuses on what's most important to the customer, not what's most important to the seller.

Closing the sale then becomes almost formulaic. Applying Smart Sales Methods, your sales team summarizes everything using our relative value closing formula, **RV = BR + RM@FMP.**

Don't let the mathematical look put you off. Relative Value, like the SEL model, is one of the main pillars of the Smart Sales Method and we'll be returning to it in more depth soon enough. In terms of the Alignment phase, what it means is that your sales team will describe how the client is achieving a desirable value closing formula, **RV = BR + RM@ FMP.** Relative Value, like the SEL model, is one of the main pillars of the Smart Sales Method and we'll be returning to it in more depth soon enough. In terms of the Alignment phase, it means that your sales team will describe how the client is achieving a desirable relative value (RV) in terms of an improved business result (BR) while ensuring that potential risks are properly mitigated or managed (RM), and that the solution being provided to the customer is at a fair market price (FMP).

And that's the overview of the Smart Sales Method deal flow.

We know: it seems counter-intuitive. You're used to seeing sales reps making hundreds upon hundreds of cold calls, trying to build personal relationships, endlessly repeating canned lists of features and benefits, submitting quotes and following up; and usually getting nowhere.

"But everyone does it!"

Which is why they're not getting results.

Yes, this is new terminology and a new method, and it will change how your sales team does things. The question is, will the change be negative or positive? How long will it take? What are the risks? What are the rewards?

We're seeing that greater than 94% of the B2B technology sales teams that implement this process significantly improve their sales results within the first 3-5 months.

The next three chapters will show you how to apply the Survey, Assess and Align steps of The Smart Sales Method.

If now or at that point you have questions, please contact me. In an initial conversation, we can determine feasibility, potential return for your organization and if The Smart Sales Method is the right fit for you.

Joe Morone

www.worldleaderssales.com
LinkedIn.com/in/increasesales
Email: jmorone@worldleaderssales.com
Mobile or text: (585) 732-5666

CHAPTER FOUR

SMART PROSPECTING

Chapter Four

To sell to a customer, you first have to connect to a customer – to connect to a decision maker that has a goal or problem that aligns to what you produce or provide.

In sales, that's called prospecting. It's absolutely fundamental to being a successful salesperson and to having a successful and thriving business.

Each sales rep working for you should have approximately three times the number of sales opportunities in their individual overall pipeline as compared to their expected annual, quarterly or monthly goal. If your pipeline of sales opportunities isn't three times your expected annual sales, consistently, you have a prospecting problem.

A healthy pipeline? That's what follows when (1) your sales reps are working with all of the correct customer decision makers; when (2) there's a strong business case for your offerings; when (3) the expected close date parallels the customers' expectations for a solution.

If you don't have a healthy pipeline, you may be wondering why. You may be asking yourself,

"Does my sales team lack the skill or will to prospect effectively"?"

Before you ask that question, you should first ask: does our organization have the right *sales methods* in place for building a healthy pipeline? Are we targeting the right market? Are we using the right message? Are we applying the right prospecting methods consistently, every day?"

We call this the "3 M's": Market. Message. Methods.

Apply them and you can correct what's going wrong.

And what exactly *is* going wrong? Most likely your sales reps are not applying what we statistically know works best. Instead you are hoping that your sales reps will find new business because of some mysterious personal "knack" or "hunger" or "charisma."

Only they don't.

So now, let's begin doing only what we can statistically *expect* to work. The entire sequence in the right order. The 3M's. Market, Message, Methods.

Let's start by addressing the right *Market.*

Step 1: Staking Your Claim

The required first step for success in prospecting is to develop a validated corporate prospecting database. That database should be the sole repository for all prospecting (and marketing) activities. You constrain prospecting activities only to customers that fit these parameters:

• The prospect is located within your targeted geography.

• The organization is part of an industry that commonly buys what you sell or have sold to.

• Contact titles are executive-level or management-level decision makers — *only*. (Prospecting by starting with Procurement is *not* part of The Smart Sales Method.)

This is where most sales organizations fall down. Rather than focusing on decision makers in companies that best align to your strengths, too many reps take an undisciplined random approach to deciding whom to involve in their prospecting functions. They try to connect through meetings, calls, emails, tweets, blog posts, LinkedIn, newsletters, teaching events, networking events, etcetera; but not to the right person.

In fact, they normally try to connect to the *wrong* people from the very start: they ask to be put through to Procurement, which doesn't have decision authority to buy, but *is* mandated to drive prices to rock bottom.

Sales reps need to have a tight, targeted list of prospects before they begin any prospecting activity. They don't necessarily have to be the ones that assemble that list. But it must be a list of *buyers* – a list of *decision makers* and *stakeholders*.

And this list should be understood to be a *corporate* asset, *not* a salesperson's asset.

Many of the sales people we re-train do what they call a "Sticky." Someone will say, "Here's a lead. Give them a call." The rep writes it down on a Sticky note, puts it on their computer screen, calls the number when he or she gets a minute, and doesn't get through. And then? Then the rep *throws the name away!*

And a valuable potential customer or contact – an asset that could be used in future prospecting functions, in networking, in information gathering – is simply and pointlessly wasted.

It now has to be a top CEO responsibility to build and hold one of the companies' most valuable assets: a validated and complete corporate sales and marketing database. That enables companies to control and maintain some of the most crucial company information possible — a full and comprehensive list of its prospective customers, now and in years to come.

Poor and ineffective company sales management lets the sales person decide whom to call — what market, what title, whatever — and lets the sales person do what they want with the information. In most situations the sales person connects with the wrong person from the start; and the sales cycle is ineffective from the start. Whichever company representative is assigned to assemble a prospect database, getting the database right first and foremost is a major company responsibility.

A good database also includes *former* clients: people that have bought from your firm before and have drifted away but could easily drift back — if contacted.

A good database also includes *recommenders*. They can be industry analysts or subject matter experts, networking group leaders or elected officials, industry journalists or industry notables that know your business and think well of it. If they're people that have influence within your prospective customer base, they need to be on your list.

Moving from random data collection to structured data collection is moving from blind stumbling in a potential market to consciously making that market or territory your own, and staking your claim to it.

Step 2: Constructing The Survival Message

We've already mentioned an exceptionally powerful tool we use in Smart Sales called the 5x1 ("Five By One"). It grabs the attention of a prospect and gets to their survival instinct literally within seconds.

But it doesn't do that if the sales rep starts out by talking about how great he or she is, or how great your offerings are. Yet sales reps do this all the time!

Why they do it is understandable. Statistical data tells us that the great majority of sales people feel they don't get the respect they feel they deserve. Years of living through rejection has left many of them feeling that they're not welcome; that they're imposing on the customer; that the customer is reluctant even to hear them out. They feel they have to earn the right to get the customer even to listen to them. So they feel that they have to "differentiate from the competition" right out of the box.

In short, they've developed some very self-limiting beliefs – beliefs and ideas that severely limit their effectiveness and drive them to use ineffective and counter-productive techniques. At our Sales Training classes we review forty-seven such self-limiting beliefs that negatively impact sales success. When you and your sales force have learned to recognize them as myths, you'll have taken a giant step to improving their outlook, performance and earning capability – and your own.

To earn the right to have your (future) customer listen, your salespeople have to discuss your customer's business needs first. You have to demonstrate a deep understanding of your customer's business challenges — perhaps better than they know it themselves.

That's why our 5x1 contact approach often starts with the sales rep saying:

"We work every day with executives or managers like you to improve _____ [*sales results, operational effectiveness, product or service quality, compliance/safety or profitability*] by providing _____ [*your offerings*]."

You open with a five-second message or provocation question about their business results that you know is important or interesting to them.

Then, when the customer says, "Who the hell are you?" you can talk about who you are and what you do.

But you don't start off by talking about yourself or your offerings. Your focus must be 100% on the *customer* and the customer's business.

The conventional approach is the complete opposite of this. Which is why it doesn't work.

Intelligent buyers (the ones that truly have business responsibility and decision authority) shun ineffective sales people like the plague. Ineffective sales people focus on relationships. Marginally effective sales people focus on why their products or services are better than the competition. Smart sales people initially focus on exactly that: enabling their customers to better compete and survive in today's business environment.

The Smart Sales rep should focus on competitive advantage for the client and on tools like the 5x1 to transition to that conversation. It's that total focus on what matters to the customer that makes the first five seconds of a conversation (verbal or written) an opportunity for a Smart Sales rep instead of a hurdle.

If in the first five seconds the sales rep is talking about themselves or your company, they're not triggering the customer's survival. If they're talking about the customer's competitive advantage in the first five seconds, right out of the box, they're connecting instantly to the listener's SEL model: they're talking about what matters.

If the sales rep can communicate to a prospect or listener that they may be able to enhance the listener's personal or company competitive advantage, that rep guarantees himself or herself a hearing.

How is it done? Simply by bringing up the subject of a relevant, valuable or critically important improvement in the course of introducing yourself. Again, the general form is this:

"We work with [*job title or company type*] to improve [*specific results*] by providing [*description of your offering*]."

Think about it. Do they want to talk to someone they don't know about a product or service they may have never heard of? Maybe, maybe not. Do they want to *improve?* To get stronger than the competition, more efficient, to generate more revenue? Who doesn't? Who wouldn't want to at least hear more?

A concrete example? Worldleaders Inc. provides sales training and recruiting. If we were to contact a prospect initially and simply say we do sales training and recruiting, the reaction would likely be, "So what? All sorts of firms do. Why should that matter to us?" But suppose we open by saying, "We work specifically with B2B technology companies to double sales in less than six months by training sales reps in the most effective statistically supported sales practices known." *Now*, if you're CEO of a B2B technology firm that wants better sales results, you pay attention. *Now* you want to know more.

Once you evoke that survival instinct, you can support it by restating it in another, equally powerful, way. You may say, "Are your sales reps bringing in all the revenue you would like?" The answer is almost certainly no, and that answer threatens the business's survival and the survival of the position of the listener in that business. Threatening survival evokes survival.

You can also support it quickly, strongly and plausibly by using benchmarks. What are benchmarks? An attainable third-party measure that shows that your suggested improvement is possible.

You start by asking, "Have you ever — ?"

"Have you ever considered measuring your sales department against industry best practices for sales results?'

'How would you compare your sales team to the top 6% in your industry?"

Benchmarking challenges the client to reach industry standards. Sometimes it allows clients to probe and match or exceed stronger competitor performance. But it's more than a simple challenge. Using third party benchmarks is a very easy way to get the customer to think about how to get more competitive or compliant in their marketplace. They're an amazingly effective way to keep the customer in their survival mode. Because the dialogue is all about the benchmark, not the sales rep.

If there *are* no ready benchmarks? Create your own, based on your success in working with your existing clients. What you can say is, "When we work with organizations like yours, operating at similar levels, we're able to bring them up by (say) 53%."

What's happening? *You* become the benchmark. It's your way of doing business that creates the benchmark. Take Apple. There was no benchmark for droids until Apple set the benchmark. Droids may actually have surpassed that benchmark, but every droid still has to meet or exceed or distinguish itself against that benchmark.

Once you bring up a benchmark, once you get them thinking about the gap between where they *are* and where they *could be* and know they *need* to be, the "E" part of the SEL model automatically kicks in. You cement that interest emotionally by asking, "Is that important or interesting to you? Why? Why now?"

Ask them why it's important and interesting to them, and you get *them* to make the arguments that will convince them. Ask them "Why now?" and you get *them* thinking about and fanning the fires of urgency!

Once you have survival and emotion operating, you transition into logic and the assessment phase by suggesting a meeting intended to determine feasibility, potential return, and best fit.

We've already shown how offering such an assessment can ease the transition from initial contact to sale. It doesn't take much to see how an offered conversation about benchmarks, competitive advantage, and potential business returns would be a conversation business stakeholders would like to have, or how quickly and totally it would distinguish the Smart Sales prospector from someone calling to ask whom to send a quote to in procurement.

But that isn't the only benefit of prospecting the Smart Sales way.

One of the biggest reasons for a sale being stalled or a decision never being made is that the selling team does not gain access or work with the all stakeholders from the buying organization.

The sales person doesn't get to the real decision

makers. We see this occur in greater than 90% of the situations where sales opportunities are not moving forward. The major difference of prospecting the Smart Sales way is that during the 5x1, a statement is made that, "When we work with organizations like yours, we include the business user because we'll be talking about making or saving money. We include the end user because we'll be discussing functionality, usability and reliability. We include procurement because we'll be discussing pricing, terms and conditions." These are the essential stakeholders that the sales person actively works to bring together.

Look at it this way. You can't sell a solution to a firm without involving the right people in the evaluation, decision or implementation processes. You don't want to. Time and again a sales person will take a single-threaded approach, selling only to procurement, seeing them as the primary decision maker, only to eventually realize that they simply are not, after a waste of weeks, months, even years.

When we at Worldleaders approach a prospect, we're not asking whether or not our sales training or sales recruiting services can help them. We *know* they can. If what you're offering is solid, and if the market you're approaching is appropriate, you know your product or service can help them too. You're not doing an assessment to establish that. What you're trying to establish if it's possible for *them* to attain that benchmark, that goal, with your help. A Fit-Assessment is there to allow you, the seller, to work with all decision makers to *qualify* that buyer. It's not about them deciding whether or not to do business with you. It's about *you* deciding if the competitive advantage you are offering can be achieved by that organization at that time.

When we prospect to do a Fit-Assessment, what we're really looking to assess is the prospect. We've already partially qualified them by the fact that they're in our database. Now we want to find out more about their capacities. If our service is training sales people, for example, the first question is: is the prospect's sales team even remotely capable of doing what they need to do? It's not whether *we* can do it. It's whether *they* can do it. The customer is being examined to establish if they can reach benchmarked criteria, not you. And since reaching that benchmark is critical to their business survival, they very much want to know.

If they can, do they qualify? Not yet. We need to look at potential return – theirs and ours. Is it worth doing for all concerned? Does it make money – for everyone involved? Is it ultimately profitable? If it isn't, there's no point in going further. If it is — let's do it!

Finally there's the question of "best fit." Best fit is about whether your organizations are suited to work well together.

Now it's hard for sales people to admit that they're not the right fit. They want that sale! But a CEO, a *business* leader, wants to know this from the start. They're too used to hearing things from weak sales teams like, "Oh, the customer doesn't like this, our price is too high, the features aren't right, we need to make these modifications and those changes and then, maybe, possibly, the customer will consider us."

The Smart Sales approach is saying, "Can the customer get to where they need to be? Is it worth doing in terms of financial return? Can we work effectively together?" What's the point of selling someone on something that can't be done, or isn't worth doing in terms of time and cost? Why not catch it straight away in an assessment that can take as little as a few hours, instead of wasting time and money dragging things out for weeks, months – sometimes years?

This is why we often refer to prospecting as "surveying." Too many sales people focus on trying to talk a customer *into* a need, whether a real need is there or not. The truth is, the best you can do is to survey a customer and learn whether they have genuine needs, or whether they're fully aware of real but non-obvious problems or needs.

Since there is always a preferred comparative state in some respect that a business would like to be in; since adapting competitively to a constantly changing environment always requires change and updating; and since important latent needs are not always clear, an assessment is always welcome. Businesses know how important serious objective assessments are to their survival, and what it can mean to their success. They welcome such assessments.

How does this affect the prospector's sales message? Profoundly.

The goal of the prospecting sales executive is to survey the potential customer to see whether they're truly desirable customers, and the Fit-Assessment ascertains that. The customer's goal is not merely to review a product, but to gain a competitive advantage that enhances their business survival – and the Fit-Assessment ascertains that, too.

The prospecting Smart Sales rep is not doing conventional prospecting at all.

He or she is not trying to contact someone at random who may or may not be interested in a one-shot purchase of a product or service. The Smart Sales rep is working to set up a mutually desirable, win-win goal: a Fit-Assessment that will demonstrate to both parties the value, or not, of going ahead with a business transaction. That changes the whole initial conversation. The *real* objective of the prospecting conversation is to sell the Fit-Assessment. That assessment will establish whether such a purchase is in everyone's best interest.

You know you've done your prospecting job well when you've set up a conversation (which could be a follow-up phone call, a Skype conference, or an on-site multi-person discussion) with your prescribed stakeholders to discuss feasibility, potential return and whether or not you're the best fit.

Great prospecting, prospecting with the highest statistical probability of success, is prospecting that communicates possible competitive advantage (through a variety of media) to potential customers, surveys them for unmet goals or unsolved problems, and offers to perform an assessment to see if an improvement in competitive advantage can be achieved.

The message is not about the sales rep, not about the firm, not even about the offering, but about the *business advantage* that an offering can provide and about arranging a discussion with the key decision makers to objectively assess and confirm that.

Step 3: Methods of Surveying Prospects for Potential Competitive Advantage

Now at this point you've got the following:

• A *validated prospecting database* of executive-level and management-level contacts from organizations that commonly buy what you sell, located within your targeted market geography.

• A *message that evokes or questions their need for a particular competitive advantage,* that shows a possible way to gain improved sales results – for example, greater operational effectiveness, higher product or service quality, better compliance/safety, enhanced profitability — as it aligns to your offerings.

The good news is that this positions you much more realistically to gain three times the pipeline as we discussed.

Instead of blindly trying to sell a product or service to a poorly understood and reluctant buyer, you're offering to provide a valuable analysis of a firm's competitive strength, and possibly a way to strengthen it even further. You've made connecting into something the buyer finds *desirable.*

That's why prospecting in a way that involving suggesting a Fit-Assessment is such a game-changer.

But to land the assessment, and make the whole prospecting process from start to finish more effective, we need to make each aspect of that process as simple for salespeople to execute as possible, just as easy for management to be able to measure, and something that can be done in a variety of effective ways and channels.

Some of the ways to do that include:

• Daily participation at select industry groups aligned to your prospecting database demographics. Ideally this should be done in person. But if you're selling regionally, nationally or internationally, it can be done virtually and online too. Prospects are industry professionals, and there are professional networks online and off. You should have your sales team participating as board members, speakers or industry experts in every applicable group.

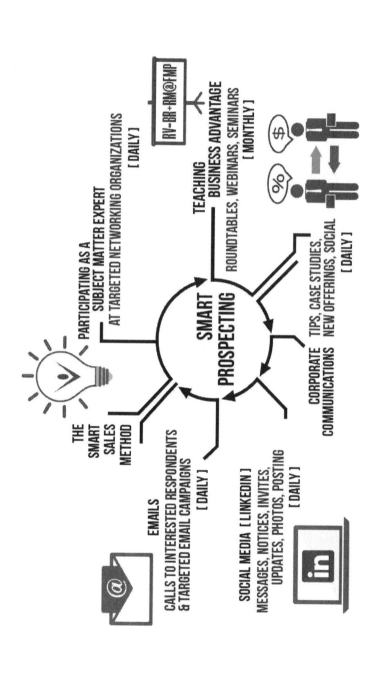

• Facilitating monthly industry teaching events and best practice forums. This can include customer roundtables, webinars, seminars, trade shows, and social events focused on teaching clients how to improve their competitive advantage. We recommend at least one such teaching event per month.

• Sending bi-weekly emails, newsletters or press releases, which can communicate tips, news, case studies and company events — relevant information that enables clients to learn more about their unique business challenges and how your organizations can assist.

• Daily social media posting and blogging. For B2B, LinkedIn is the single best venue. (Your sales team must have a LinkedIn presence and an accurate LinkedIn profile that describes them as an industry expert.)

When your sales people are networking daily, sending out newsletters and other information biweekly, and providing teaching events monthly, they won't have to depend on outreach to find business. Your best prospects will be connecting to *you*, and connecting on a daily basis. All of this activity, done effectively, in the order and volume described, will serve to position you, your sales team and your organization as an industry expert – possibly *the* industry experts.

Making Contact

And when it comes to actually making contact?

First, let's end the debate about cold call versus emailing versus social media. Which works best? They all work. A good sales rep has them all in their tool kit and uses every one every day. A good sales rep uses them all in an integrated way.

Next, let's forget about building "relationships" during the prospecting part of the sale. The statistics show flatly that this is among the least effective approaches.

Somewhat effective sales people focus on why their product and/or service is better than competitors.

Smart Sales people focus on helping customers see how that product best helps the buyer's business to compete.

Your prospect will be glad to have a relationship with someone that advances his or her business. Contribute nothing of value to that business and the relationship won't last long.

Above all, salespeople have to overcome the destructive practice of throwing away the critically important initial first few seconds of a call by talking about themselves.

And once these new approaches and techniques are in place? Once your sales people are connecting to the real decision makers? What's happens then?

The Smart Fit-Assessment – described next in close-up detail.

CHAPTER FIVE

SMART
FIT-
ASSESSMENTS

Chapter Five

The objective of a Fit-Assessment is to capture and develop the complete and accurate business and technical requirements needed for constructing a compelling proposal – a proposal that provides a unique and persuasive business return for both parties.

When the Fit-Assessment is performed correctly, with the correct participants, statistically the probability of achieving a sale approaches 70%.

Why is it so effective? What takes place? Who takes part? What are the dynamics? In what order do things happen? Now that we've gotten the assessment to take place, what actually happens?

In a Fit-Assessment, one of your goals is to position your organization as a thought leader in the client's industry – to be recognized as a subject matter expert, as *the* subject matter experts in their industry, as the people most qualified to help them improve their business performance.

Studies tell us that B2B clients buy from those they consider to be the thought leaders more than any other evaluation factor. This includes factors like brand, product performance, price and relationships.

How do you demonstrate thought leadership? By asking, or having your sales team ask and intelligently address, a very specific set of questions. Ask the right questions, in the right order, and your customer will quickly begin to understand that you've done this many times before; that you understand their situation completely, and that you can lead them quickly, efficiently and exactly to their goal.

In the prospecting step, described in the previous chapter, we learned how to survey a prospect for interest or need in order to reach a defined ideal state or benchmark important to their business and professional survival.

In this step we're not assessing that target goal; we're not even assessing our ability to help them get there. We're assessing the *customer's* ability to get there.

When you facilitate a Smart Sales Fit-Assessment, your team is looking at the *customer's* readiness and ability to achieve their ideal state or benchmark. Not the other way around. The selling firm's ability to deliver is assumed. It's a given. That's what you do for a living. That's why you're the subject matter experts. That's how you know the right questions to ask. What you're trying to find out is whether *they* can measure up.

The second objective of a Smart Sales Fit-Assessment involves bringing together the key people on the buyer and seller side of the equation – on the buyer side, specifically those who are most likely to be affected by and responsible for making the buying decision.

Once these key people are brought together, how does the Fit-Assessment progress?

By means of a question and answer discussion involving all the key players.

Remember, during the 5x1, you used the statement, "When we work with organizations like yours, we include the business user because we will be discussing a business result. We include the end user because we will be discussing functionality, usability and reliability. We include procurement because we'll be discussing pricing and terms and conditions." (This is how you brought together the true decision-makers.)

First, you assess the expected business and technical impact. What will happen if the proposed solution or offering is implemented? What outcome can be expected? What will improve? What possible risks or disruptions may occur, and how can those risks or disruptions be mitigated?

Next, you review solutions previously considered, and the reasons why they were not used. This includes internal solutions and ideas from external partners.

Then, you evaluate technical and feasibility constraints that could potentially become barriers in the short term and in the long term.

Next, you discuss potential competing client

priorities in terms of their management attention, resources, time or budget.

Then, you identify any important timelines, including time-to-advantage, provider selection, and evaluation and proposal due dates.

Next, you analyze budget allocation and/or the requirements for budget justification.

Finally, you confirm selection criteria with each stakeholder to ensure that you are aligning the solution specifically to their needs, constraints and timing.

And so, ideally, the process leads everyone to that ideal end state where both the buyers and sellers see clearly that the solution criteria does exactly what the customer needs it to do.

How effective is it? Statistics say that 68% of buyers who reach this stage go on to close. In our own experience, 70% or more is the general closing rate on the following Smart Proposal.

Is it important or interesting to you to turn almost three out of four sales discussions with clients into agreements to buy?

This is how you get there.

In a Fit-Assessment you are assessing whether your offerings can secure a specific business advantage for your customer. To do that you will be asking a specific set of questions positioned in a specific order. We'll get to those specific questions in a moment. Right now we want to caution you to not

– we repeat, *not* -- ask random, open-ended questions that may or may not align to what you're selling.

Please: do *not* ask them what keeps them "up at night," what their "pain" is, what you "have to do to earn their business!"

A Fit-Assessment is *not* a product presentation. Under no circumstances should it turn into the sales team talking about your products or services.

You are assessing the *customer* and *their* capacity to implement your solution. You will be much more successful at presenting once you have a complete business and technical understanding of the overall business and technical objective.

Nothing is more disruptive, or destructive to an ultimate sale, than a disguised attempt at presenting during a Fit-Assessment.

In a Fit-Assessment you want to keep the customer focused totally on *their* unmet goal or unsolved problem. When sales people make the mistake of trying to be overly social during the Fit-Assessment, it lessens the impact and concentration on the customer's gap between their current state and the ideal state.

At this stage, stay focused on their business.

The Assessment Questions

What questions specifically do you ask, and in what order, during the flow of the assessment?

The following questions are a guideline that

we recommend. You may have additional technical questions that you may need to ask afterwards. That's fine. It's not unusual to contact members on the buying side after the assessment and get their further input as you craft the proposal – in fact we strongly recommend it!

But at this point there are under a dozen questions you will need to ask and to have answered. The questions we suggest you ask are these:

1. How would this impact your business positively?

2. What potential drawbacks, risks or disruptions may be involved? Please describe them.

3. Why is this important now?

4. What are the ramifications of delaying or doing nothing?

5. What is the ideal timing?
   a. When will the project or installation or delivery need to be completed?
   b. When will you select the appropriate supplier?
   c. When is the proposal due?

6. What solutions have been previously considered? Please describe them. (And are they internally

provided solutions, externally recommended or suggested by third parties?)

7. Do you have any competing priorities for your management attention, resources, time or budget? Please describe them.

8. Do you face any potential constraints – physical, environmental, technical, skill-related, compliance-related? Please describe them.

9. What are your views as to technical feasibility?

10. Is this budgeted, or does it require budget justification?

11. What are the acceptance criteria for each stakeholder or decision-maker?
> a. Business (make or save money, meet compliance)
> b. User (capability, usability, reliability)
> c. Financial (price, budget, discounts)

If you had complete and accurate answers to all of these questions, what do you think your number of closings would be?

There's no need to guess. In our experience, the answer is approximately three out of four.

70% or more is the general closing rate we see with a Smart Proposal.

Working with the Right Decision Makers

Important as the questions are, no less important is *always* ensuring that the sales executive has brought in the right decision makers (business, user and financial level decision makers) to participate in the Fit-Assessment. We *cannot* emphasize this strongly enough. If these three stakeholders are not involved, the Fit-Assessment takes a severe loss in terms of effectiveness.

Why, and why specifically those three stakeholders, at those three levels?

We need to have the business level stakeholder involved when we perform this level of assessment because we need to talk about their business objectives, and how the initiative impacts their business or operational competitiveness. In other words, how they will make or save more money.

We also need to have user-level representation involved because we need to discuss technical aspects involving capability, usability and reliability.

We need to have procurement involved because cost is involved, and we want to be sure that what needs to be done can be done at a fair market price.

That's why we want to have those people from each of these areas involved in the discussion.

That's also exactly the way we need to explain it to them when positioning and scheduling a Fit-Assessment.

Again: that's *exactly* what we ought to do, in those words, to the customer.

We are not asking who should be involved, we are describing to the customer who *must* be involved and why.

Your proposed solution can only be as accurate as your understanding of the full picture. In order to fully understand the complete and accurate business and technical requirements, we need to involve the people most closely involved: the stakeholders from their business, user and financial leadership team.

Their presence assures an accurate assessment. And because a Smart Fit-Assessment is a bi-directional conversation, it allows the buyers, and you the subject matter experts, to work together, iterate, and clearly work out objectives, barriers, variations and costs.

Bringing these key members of the customer team together is also critically important because it brings together what in many cases is a buying team that *may not recognize themselves as such.* Because in many cases the customers *themselves* don't actually know who within their organization is or should be involved in a buying decision, and exactly what that decision should be based on. Companies themselves typically do not have a formally assigned buying team.

But you, the seller, know that a high enough business level company official will actively want to see a business advantage, and may have authority to authorize a deal directly; that a procurement official will be needed to provide input; that those in the company using or affected by the solution will also have input to provide that is critical to enabling a sale.

Assemble these individuals and you have in effect assembled a buying team. Fail to assemble them, and you will be talking to a group that has only a limited authority to buy – if any. Failing to do this is why so many sales cycles are lasting as long as eighteen months, and why approximately 40% of them end with no decision made at all, resulting in a tremendous waste of time and money for both the buyer and the seller.

Time and again we see the client's internal assessment process being inconsistently performed by the wrong stakeholders. Purchases are proposed and even made with little or no alignment to an expected business result, with no plan for risk mitigation, with no consideration of relative value or comparison to a fair market price.

Simply *raising* those issues gains more credibility and stature for your selling team, as opposed to the usual endless product and price comparisons that say nothing whatever about the potential *business impact* of a sale.

That's why it's so important for the Smart Sales team to facilitate a Smart Fit-Assessment with the correct members of the client's organization.

Does it seem counterintuitive for you the seller to actively select your buyers? What's *really* counterintuitive is to try to get buying decisions and commitments the way conventional sales people do – from those who *don't* make the decisions, *don't* have a stake in the outcome, and who have no *authority* to commit. These three stakeholder titles are the critical ones, and they're also the ones most likely to be affected by the right or wrong buying decision. They're not simply the ones *we* want to be there. They're the ones who *themselves* most want to be there.

Does it seem strange that many businesses

don't know who makes, or how they make, their own internal decisions for buying innovation or new technology? It's a fact. Any number of capital projects fails simply because of lack of internal project ownership, inadequate or incomplete requirements, and poor implementation planning.

A strong business case that is accurate and complete, and *not known* by the relevant stakeholders and decision-makers, is worthless.

Differentiation is no longer primarily about products or services: it's about demonstrating best overall product or service fit to business, technical and financial stakeholders.

And to demonstrate it to them, they have to *be* there.

If the only thing you take away from this chapter is the *absolute necessity* to involve the relevant business, user and financial stakeholders in a Fit-Assessment, you'll have taken a giant step forward in doing it exactly right.

The Sales Team

But getting the right names, titles and roles on the buyer side involved isn't the whole story. Putting the right sales team together is just as critical. A successful Fit-Assessment requires a special combination of people on the selling side of the equation.

Who needs to be on that team?

The sales representative, a sales engineering

person and an executive-level sponsor.

The sales representative is responsible for facilitating the overall discussion. This involves scheduling, facilitating the Smart Fit-Assessment, ensuring that all questions are prepared and asked and answered correctly by all members of the buying and selling team, and most importantly that the Align step (the presentation of the Smart Proposal) is scheduled, and that all members commit to being present at that presentation.

The sales engineer is responsible for ascertaining complete and accurate business and technical requirements. This is a key role that is often overlooked or misunderstood. Statistically we know that effective sales engineering and solution alignment represents greater than 50% of the overall win factor.

This is because the client almost always looks to the sales engineer as the person that they can go back to if something goes wrong. The sales engineer speaks with full technical expertise, and is the person that will have to deal with things if the solution implementation doesn't work out or needs correction. The sales engineer wants that fit to be right, and to be right the first time, and can best tell if it's technically possible; and the buyer knows it.

The buyer has considerable respect for the sales engineer – for this reason alone, sales engineering people should be fully trained and highly competent in Smart Sales Methods and skills.

Last but very far from least, it is *critically* important to include an executive sponsor on the selling team during the assessment. This is someone who is at peer level with the business level stakeholder on the buying side. If you're the business leader, this could be you. It *must* be you in major sales opportunities.

During a Fit-Assessment, your role as an executive sponsor is very simple. You are there (physically, online or over the phone) to audit the process and make sure that you and the business level stakeholders agree as to the objectives, and that you both are committing resources from your respective organizations to work openly for the purpose of proper due diligence.

You are also there because, like the sales engineer, you stand high in the estimation of the key decision maker on the buyers' team – a business level executive like yourself. Trust and credibility are always elements of a buying situation, and decisions to buy flow more easily when the discussions are peer-to-peer.

When and if a solution is presented during the Alignment or presentation stage of the Smart Sales Method, your role will become more significant.

We'll discuss this in more detail in the next chapter.

The Role Dynamics of the Fit-Assessment

The key issue during a Fit-Assessment is how

things look from the customer's point of view.

The business-level decision-maker is looking for a business solution.

The user-level decision-maker is looking for capability, usability and reliability.

The procurement-level decision-maker is looking at price versus specifications.

The business level stakeholder is going to be looking very closely at the person in the sales engineering role, much more closely than at the sales person, because the business level stakeholder knows that the sales engineer is the one responsible for designing the solution. They know that if they buy, that engineer will likely be involved with delivering that solution. *And so what the engineer says carries significant weight and credibility.*

Because of this, at some point during the Fit-Assessment it's smart to have the sales engineer step up and take a leadership role. Because what the highest-level decision maker on the customer side is looking for is how strong that sales engineer is, and how strong they're likely to be after the sale.

They know the sales person is going to go away to sell other customers. What they *want* to know is, who's going to stay behind and actually make that offering work? Who will be *delivering* the solution, not selling it?

It's going to be the engineer. And most sales people are not fully aware of this or fully appreciate how important it is. They often don't want the sales engineer to go into too much detail or say anything that can be construed as negative about the product or solution. They'll actually tell the sales engineer, "*Don't* do this, don't do that, and don't say too much." When the truth is, the customer *loves* that display of expertise, that geekiness, that level of candidness.

The problem is, the sales engineer doesn't always know how to take the customer to the next step. They don't know how to advance or close the sale. They *are* critical in bringing the customer *closer* to that close, however. And in a Fit-Assessment situation, the sales person is just not as well positioned to do that; not as effective as the sales engineer, or even the executive sponsor.

Why not? For one thing, they're not seen as objective. The sales person's salary or commission is tied into whether or not the sale is made. The sales engineer's isn't. The customer knows the sales person wants that sale and probably wants it badly, and the customer is worried that the sales person may want it badly enough to make a case that's stronger than the reality.

But the sales engineer will be up front. They're not going to inflate what the solution can do: they're going to be the ones actually implementing it.

And when the buyer looks across the table and see another CEO or business leader?

That works too. That other C-level person is in their shoes. They can trust that person. The CEO of a technology company selling to them is a colleague —

a peer. To that customer, the sales engineer and the CEO/business leader are wearing the white hats, not the black hats.

The customer enters the discussion with an already existing respect for those two people. So those two people should be up front and prominent during the assessment. Having them present at the presentation is your best option. It's Smart Selling.

And it's especially smart when that sales engineer and that CEO are familiar with the Smart Sales Method. The Smart Sales Method gives them systematic sales knowledge and sales capabilities on top of their technical or leadership skills – something valuable in any employee.

We're emphasizing the importance of giving the sales engineer and executive sponsor active roles, because it's so effective and disarming.

But this doesn't mean sales people have no role during a Fit-Assessment. Far from it.

A sales person must facilitate the entire assessment. We mentioned this earlier, but what exactly does this mean? How is it done? Why is it important?

We can best describe the facilitator role by simply stating the definition: "A facilitator helps a group of people understand their common objectives and assists them to plan how to achieve these objectives." In doing so, the facilitator remains "neutral" – he or she stands back, and doesn't take a particular position in the discussion.

Smart Fit-Assessments are much more authentic and effective when each participant stays within the boundaries of their assigned roles. As discussed, the salesperson facilitates the assessment, the sale engineering person leads the client through the business and technical requirements involved during the assessment, and the executive sponsor ensures that proper due diligence is taking place.

When this comes together, the customer recognizes that industry experts are working with their team for an objective and honest best-fit solution. This is true thought leadership.

Even people who get this sometimes miss it. They think, "Wow, what a great way of getting the customer to believe we actually care." No. The best way to give that impression is to *actually* care — to reduce the amount of "selling" in a Fit-Assessment to absolute *zero*, to let the facts speak so clearly that the facts make the sale. Again, only leadership ensures that.

The credibility of a sales team can be so strong during a Smart Fit-Assessment that the sale may be made even before the solution is presented. We've seen it happen – times when the Fit-Assessment is so well executed that the solution is clearly identified in the course of it, and the deal is closed right there.

Why not? When the right stakeholders from both sides are working together and the right questions are being asked, and expertise is evident and transparent, a decision to move forward immediately will become just plain obvious.

But can we really consider the sale closed at that point?

Or do we still need to keep going forward, step by deliberate step?

Keep reading and learn the most statistically supported answer.

Closing on Relative Value:
RV=BR+RM@FMP

How many times have you heard these statistically un-supported clichés?

"It's all about value!"

"It's all about the lowest price!"

"It's all about relationships!"

You either have to have the best offering or be the lowest price. If you don't, you better be most liked. Almost every salesperson, sales manager or sales trainer believes that some combination of these elements is the real story of why clients buy. Despite the fact that studies show these to be the least effective sales approaches.

Once your sales team has completed a Smart Fit-Assessment, they will likely have all the valid information needed to develop an effective proposal.

But having the information and pulling it together into a compelling and persuasive summary that drives a buyer to close are two different things.

That summary is a simple statement or statements that are not solely about the product or service or price, but demonstrate the business return that the product delivers, describes how potential risks are mitigated, and shows how this is achieved at a fair market price. The sales team presents it in an equation: $RV = BR + RM@FMP$.

This formula explains Relative Value and states that the relative value of a solution is described by the *Business Return* it provides (profit, revenue, savings), explains how any acquisition *Risk* (contractual, performance, reliability and schedule) is addressed and *Mitigated*, and shows that the solution is being offered at a *Fair Market Price.*

A Fit-Assessment is a conversation – on-site or even via conference call – in which your sales team, and stakeholders you have brought together from the buyer's firm, assess *not* whether your product is cheaper than a competing product, but whether your solution or offering can (1) gain the buyer an agreed upon business advantage, (2) whether your offering mitigates any related risks, and (3), whether these advantages are being offered at a competitive industry price. The Relative Value formula keeps the conversation and the customer focused on those advantages.

In the next chapter, and in the final steps of the Smart Sales Method, we are going to cover how to construct your Smart Proposal and align your specific Relative Value solution to the exact needs of your customer. We call this the Align step because it enables you to align your solution specifically to your customer's environment, in a document that conclusively demonstrates feasibility, business return and best fit.

Then finally we will present and close using a tool that experience has shown us is the most effective and deliberate closing approach now available: Relative Value.

Note: this book was written to be a guideline for CEOs and Leaders of B2B technology sales teams that sell a complex product within a very competitive environment. We did everything possible to simplify the Survey and Assessments steps within the Smart Sales Method. But at the same time we know you may want to talk through these concepts. It's for this reason, that we offer our contact information to you. Please feel free to call, text or email at any time. We would be happy to answer questions or walk you through the concepts.

Joe Morone

www.worldleaderssales.com
LinkedIn.com/in/increasesales
Email: jmorone@worldleaderssales.com
Mobile or text: (585) 732-5666

CHAPTER SIX

SMART PROPOSALS

Chapter Six

Some proposals win deals.

Most don't.

Why not? Because most proposals are talking all about the seller, not the customer. About themselves, not about the customer's business objectives.

The organization writing the proposal always claims to have the highest quality offerings at the lowest price. Their offerings are always described as cutting edge and second to none. Their service is always unparalleled. Their people are always the most honest and the friendliest. Sound familiar? It should be. You've heard it often enough. And you didn't believe it then, either.

How does any of that help a determined business stakeholder, technology user or financial stakeholder improve their market share, reduce working time, advance quality, meet compliance or improve profitability?

It doesn't.

The conventional proposal does not effectively address the buyers' personal or professional *survival.* Nor does the conventional proposal showcase relative value. It doesn't describe the business return, it doesn't explain how risk on the part of the buyer is mitigated, it doesn't say why the price is a reasonable price reflecting fair market value. Any parts that do touch on that, the most important parts, are either lost or buried on page nine or ten, or missing completely.

The Smart Proposal is a tool designed to enable your sales team to *win sales*. To win sales, your proposal has to go straight to relative value (RV). It needs to describe business return (BR), risk management (RM), and fair market price (FMP) immediately and powerfully, right from the start.

When you assemble your Smart Proposal correctly this way and present it properly, the numbers say your close rate should be greater than 70%.

A Smart Proposal should be as powerful and succinct as it is possible to be. You'll be able to put it into two pages. You'll be able to present it in about five minutes.

Getting the content right isn't a problem: 100% of what you've captured in the Smart Fit-Assessment can be plugged directly into the Smart Proposal. What you learn in the Smart Fit-Assessment aligns directly with what you put into the Smart Proposal.

This chapter will walk you through the Smart Proposal structure from start to finish. We'll show you why the elements are what they are, and we'll show you how you can build each part to strike with maximum impact.

At first glance a Smart Proposal looks like the complete reverse of a typical proposal. And that's absolutely correct.

The Smart Proposal, like all of our work, is built on the SEL model. That model acknowledges that the customer's personal and professional survival is the primal motivational driver for all decision makers. A Smart Proposal addresses this immediately in your Business Objectives section, and again in the second section, Alternate Strategies Considered.

Addressing survival triggers buyer emotion. After all, why do business objectives *matter* to buyers? Because the survival of their business and their professional survival depends on those objectives. Decision makers *feel* something as they consider decisions that puts their jobs and their livelihood at risk, or may open them to great new opportunity. It could be rage, terror, grief, loathing, vigilance, amazement, admiration, or joy. It could be some combination of the above, or it could flip from one feeling to another.

Whichever it is, that sense of emotional importance will drive the person feeling it to *do* something. It will trigger a sense that they need to *act* and they need to act *now*. That emotion will be followed by a search for a logical justification to do something – such as make a purchase – and this logical element is addressed in the Solutions Overview section.

So the Smart Proposal is "the reverse proposal."

THE SMART SALES PROPOSAL SEQUENCE

01. BUSINESS OBJECTIVES
02. ALTERNATE STRATEGIES CONSIDERED
03. SOLUTION OVERVIEW
04. PRICING, TERMS AND CONDITIONS
05. UNIQUELY QUALIFIED
06. COMPANY OVERVIEW

It begins with a one-line Introduction that tells them what you're going to tell them, and that lets them know that they're going to be reading a document that's all about what matters most to them. The entire SEL model is accomplished within the first page of the Smart Proposal and can be presented to your customer within the very first minute or two of the conversation.

Let's look at it section by section:

Section 1 – Business Objectives

The Business Objectives section comes first and shows you fully addressing all of the decision makers' business objectives discussed during your Smart Fit-Assessment.

It's essential here to get your client's *direct quotes*. You opened the Fit-Assessment by pointing to a benchmark or describing an achievable ideal state or business objective, and then you asked them, "How this would impact your business?" You listened to their answer. They told you what matters most to them. This is where you record it.

When the decision makers see their direct quotes on their proposal, when they hear their own words, they will know that you understand – that you fully grasp their objectives and needs. *Your* words may be impeachable: *their* words are unimpeachable. They're not going to disagree with themselves. You don't need to embroider what they say, or come up with a more elaborate or technical way of describing it. You want to re-state their needs and words *exactly* as they said it, exactly as you captured it during the Fit-Assessment. You will be reflecting back perfectly the input they gave.

And that's what makes it so powerful. This gets rid of all the fat, the spin, the false creativity, and brings it straight down to the customers themselves and their core goals and concerns – *their* need to meet an ideal state, competitive benchmark, or new business objective.

And when we say "him or her," we mean every individual decision-maker involved. In a Smart Proposal, everyone counts or no one counts. Everyone's had his or her say. Everyone sees it written down. Everyone's on board.

Section 2 –
Alternate Strategies Considered

The Alternate Strategies Considered section is designed to prevent put-offs or stalls.

At some point in every sales cycle, someone from the customer's organization will try to maintain the status quo. They will (rightfully) ask the decision makers, "Why do we need to do this now?"

And if you show them why they need to do it now, they'll go, "Why can't our own people do this?"

And when everyone agrees that it's obvious that

their own people can't do it, they'll say, "Why can't we use our existing provider? They've been good to us for twenty years. Some of them come to our annual Christmas party!"

This is the often the point where your biggest and best sales opportunities fall apart before your very eyes. "It was in the bag! It was 99.999% closed, it was a done deal!" I know. I've been there too many times myself.

Don't worry. We shouldn't be especially surprised, upset or angry when it happens. Because it always happens.

Besides, these questions are good and proper due diligence. They demonstrate reasonable buying behavior from a smart customer. And we all want smart customers. So instead of getting upset when questions like these occur, let's anticipate them and prepare for them and be ready to answer them. Let's expect them and use that expectation pro-actively to help our customer make smart decisions every time.

Remember: you've already asked these questions, and you already have the right answers. All you have to do is list your questions from the Fit-Assessment, and provide the answers that the customers themselves already gave you. It's that easy.

And when you do, you increase your probability of winning that sale tremendously, and save yourself possibly months, possibly years, of waiting, uncertainty and anguish.

The first part of the Alternate Strategies section, Take No Action, addresses this directly – and cites the answers gathered in the Fit-Assessment.

Why do we need to act now? "Because if we don't do it now, we'll lose market share this year to ABC Company." Or "If we can't become more compliant by Q4, we're going to be hit with penalties that will cripple us." Or "Because we're losing $14K per day of profit due to distribution issues."

We describe the "Why now?" in terms of making or saving more money, meeting safety and security compliance, or potentially gaining or losing market share.

Why do they need to take action? Because if they take no action, if they just keep doing what they're doing, nothing will get any better. And they might get worse.

It's a strategy that allows you to remind them that they want and need to take action and they want and need to take it *now*.

The second alternative strategy question you address is, "Why can't our own people do this? Why do we need to bring in outside people?"

Lots of reasons. Their internal resources may be tied up on other mission-critical initiatives. They may not have expertise or a track record of success for doing what needs to be done. Their internal team may not have the time, the skills, the experience, and the qualifications to be considered a workable alternative. Sometimes we even see cases where an organization will assign the work internally just because they're trying to keep unassigned people busy! This isn't a good business decision: it's a good will gesture – the kind of gesture few businesses can support any more in our current competitive business landscape. We simply no longer have the money to burn or the resources to waste.

The third alternate strategy question is, "Why can't we use our existing provider? Why do we need these new folks?"

If their current provider has the skills, experience and track record to provide the products or services effectively and within fair market pricing, they *should* go with them. But it makes no business sense to go with an existing provider if a better-fit alternative is available. Not to make the best possible decision for the company hurts the company. It threatens its business survival. And that threatens the professional survival of everyone in the company.

In today's competitive business environment, business decisions must be made with the sole criteria of engaging the best-fit provider for a specific task or product at fair market price. Anything less is irresponsible and unethical. Business and governmental agencies no longer have the competitive leeway or moral right to buy inferior products or maintain inaccurate or under-performing suppliers.

How do you say this to your customer without sounding harsh or without appearing to disrespect your competition?

Say it just the way I did above.
Exactly as is.
Verbatim.

Now stop for just a second, and think about the tremendous amount of ground you've covered in just the first one to two minutes. You're barely down the first half of the first page, and you've got their survival down. You know what their needs are. They've said so, in so many words, and in their *own* words. They know they can't wait. They know that they need to act. They know their internal team can't do it or provide it. They know existing providers can't do it or provide it.

And now they are looking to you for that solution.

So what do you do?
You provide it.

Section 3 – Solution Overview

In the Solution Overview section, you describe the solution as it aligns with the customer's business objectives as quoted in the Business Objectives section.

The best and highest probability for success is to break it down into three descriptors, in the following order:

Capability — how it works, what it will do, and how that meets the business objective.

Usability — ease of use; how well the user will interact or engage with it.

Reliability — how it will hold up under working or expected conditions.

Anytime you're selling a technical product, service or solution there's going to be a combination of those three elements: capability, usability, and reliability.

Do the full technical specifications need to be rolled out here? No.

Should they be available if the customer wants them? Of course.

But they're in the background – available, but not up front. You can present it bundled along with your Smart Proposal, but the objective is to present the solution in two pages in roughly five minutes.

The greater the complexity, the shorter and simpler you need to present it. Not the opposite. That's why everything in the Smart Proposal is condensed into simple and *decisionable* information.

Your Smart Proposal is focused not just on what the solution is, but also on what it means for the customer. The focus is not on how wonderful your solution is in isolation, but on how it generates a positive business return that makes their company stronger, and makes the decision makers' position in the company stronger.

We generally recommend that you show that positive return visually. Often a graphic or picture can show the business impact clearly, simply and powerfully, and allow the attendee or reader to see the tangible physical reality of your solution.

The Solution Overview also includes the Schedule, Deliverables and Acceptance Criteria. These now begin to address the risk management component of our Relative Value equation, **RV=BR+RM@FMP**.

The schedule, deliverables and acceptance criteria show your customer how you have managed their risk for them, including contract, performance and reliability risks.

The customer now has assurances of *what* they're going to get, *when* they're going to get it, and what their *criteria* is for considering that delivery acceptable — what the customer will sign off on, once it arrives.

So now we've covered the business return and risk management parts of the Relative Value equation.

Next? We have to communicate our commitment to, and the customer's benefit from, fair market pricing.

Section 4 – Price

Statistics show plainly that price represents only a small part – 9%, as we've said – of the B2B or B2G purchasing decision. It shouldn't be something to avoid or put off discussing, much less fear. It should be addressed early, discussed often with your customer throughout the sales cycle, and negotiated comfortably and with ease.

Your proposal should absolutely *not* be the first time your customer learns of the price range or estimated cost. Any other belief or approach works against you over time.

You don't agree? Let's take a closer look.

Price is something conventional proposals usually bury on the last page. In very small print. This is in an attempt to build value first before discussing price. We understand the logic of that, and we agree that it has some merit.

But ask yourself this. When you're shopping and you see something you like, what is the first question you ask the salesperson? "How much does it cost?" How do you react when they can't or *won't* tell you the price? We're sure you've been on the receiving end of the "Don't talk price till you build value" tactic before. You didn't like it, do you? You felt manipulated. You lost trust. You thought to yourself, "What are they hiding?"

Face it. In today's internet-savvy buying environment, finding a ballpark industry figure is just not that hard to do. People in your industry have a rough idea of what the range of prices is. Trying to hide it isn't just pointless: it destroys trust and credibility and builds resentment from your customer.

By discussing price early, often and with ease, you now have a process for effectively discussing and developing a Relative Value equation with your customer – a way to discuss price in terms of the business returns it will generate and the business risks it reduces, and a way to present it as reasonably priced overall as compared to the alternatives.

So when your customer tells you at closing time that your proposal is grossly overpriced and that you're thirty percent over the next competitor, just ask this question:

"Do you feel we missed an unexpected budgetary constraint or some other factor when calculating your Relative Value?"

In other words, is the value of the business return they're gaining from your solution greater than the cost, or not? Is the value of the business risks being mitigated greater than the price you're asking, or not? Is the price in line with other fair market prices for similar business returns and risk mitigations or not?

If the answers are that it is, then it's clearly in their interest to pay your price, *whatever* that price may be.

Most sales people think of price in only two ways: highest quality or lowest cost. The reality is that buyers pay what they consider to be a fair price for whatever fits their current situation and circumstances and needs. It's not a matter of top dollar or bottom line. It's a nuanced and flexible decision driven by multiple considerations.

The relative value formula finally puts you in a position to engage in a fair and balanced negotiation that profits everyone.

Section 5 – Uniquely Qualified

Any offering that's been tailored to best fit your customer's unique requirements is a uniquely qualified offering.

After all, you've modified your offering to achieve explicit and unique business objectives. It fulfills unique scheduling and timing requirements. It's sized to meet unique budgetary parameters. It aligns with your customer's unique technology and integrates with their unique business environment and standards.

A subsequent competitor simply cannot provide the same offering. It becomes impossible to do an apples-to-apples-style comparison.

By using a Fit-Assessment to develop your offering, proper due diligence has been completed. There's no longer any requirement to bid it out.

The term "unique" has a special meaning, and it's written into most modern procurement rules today. It was originally used as a justification for why something doesn't have to go out for competitive bid. Meaning that if a procurement organization, an end user, or a business level stakeholder recognizes a product, service or combination of the two as being unique, they can source it directly – buy it straight out, and not have to bid it.

("Uniquely Qualified" may have a special technical meaning to procurement, but don't underestimate how powerful using the phrase is within any purchasing discussion. The Smart Proposal is designed to enable you and your customer the ability to co-create uniquely qualified offerings. To many buyers, if you're uniquely qualified, you *are* best fit.)

Any one of the six points listed below can justify the seller as uniquely qualified, and therefore rightly allows them to step outside the bidding process.

We recommend that you utilize all six points, sequentially, and use every justification possible, to enable you to position your solution as strongly as possible.

The first important point to make is that you've got a product or a service that is *superior* to other competitors.

In one concise sentence, state plainly why that is.

The second positions that product as unique when you modify or *customize* it to the customer's specific needs.

The third describes being able to meet a *specific schedule or time frame*. That too can distinguish a product or services as unique.

Then there's *price*.

The price you give to them can be some level of discount from the list price. That alone makes it unique.

The *technical alignment* items will show how your product fits in with their other technology, or in their technical environment.

And then there's *cultural alignment*. How will what you're doing align to their business or their corporate culture? Why can we expect your two companies to mesh smoothly?

Section 6 – Corporate Overview

Finally we get to the part most failed proposals start with.

Corporate Overview.

There are just a few things to remember at this point.

First, keep it *short*.

Everything you've said in the preceding sections has captured the buyers' attention, presented them with a unique and compelling solution at a fair market price, and given them reason to act now.

There's nothing wrong with briefly stating your credentials.

But remember that what you're describing in the corporate overview is not so much your corporation but rather your corporation's ability to support the solution.

So describe your company skills and specialties *as they align* to this specific solution.

Define your experiences delivering similar solutions successfully.

List all of the accomplishments, awards, recognition and references that are relevant to that solution.

Then put down your keyboard or pencil.

Congratulations. You're done.

At least, you're done with the first draft. And it's important to remember that the first draft isn't the end of the story. Yes, you can do multiple drafts. No one's stopping you. More important than that, you can go through each draft with the stakeholders, and bring them into the drafting process too. Why not? At this point they're used to working with you. You've impressed them with your subject matter mastery in the Fit-Assessment. You've clarified a solution for them, and you've qualified them as being able to reach a desirable and profitable competitive benchmark. They *want* the Smart Proposal to be right on target. Of course they'll help.

Should you involve them? It's not mandatory. But there's no reason you shouldn't, and several reasons you may want to. After all, they've already worked with you to capture all the information you need during the assessment, and if there's necessary information you don't have, now's the time to get it.

You plan on having them as a client for a long time, right? Start working together now! The more development you can do together, the better.

Should you involve all three stakeholders in its development? Again, yes. Everyone counts, or no one counts. We're not just working with the business user. We're working with all three stakeholders all the time. Don't appear to be leaving anyone out of the process. Ideally you want balanced support from all of them, not one enthusiastic person dragging along unenthusiastic others. They'll all be on board, if you've done the Fit-Assessment properly and have addressed, and continue to address, everyone's concerns.

Rest assured that when you put this proposal in front of most customers, they will be impressed right away — if not outright amazed. Most corporate decision makers have never seen anything remotely resembling this lean, clean, straight-to-the-point, fact driven document.

Ideally your finished proposal will come to no more than two pages. We strive to make it one sentence per point, so you'll have cut through all the guff, all the hype, all the baloney, and focus on the *customer's advantage* with diamond-like focus. Every last fact needs to demonstrate why your firm and your solution is the one best suited and best fitted to give them exactly what *they* want and what *they* need *now*.

The discipline it takes to build that concise a two-page proposal isn't easy. But it is invaluable. When you focus only on the most important elements, when you shave it down to exactly what you need and nothing more, it trains you to understand what you're doing better, to present it better, and to close the deal better. The objective is to win the sale, yes; but also to win with ease. To win consistently.

Developing the Smart Proposal helps you learn not just how to win that one sale, but how to win many more to come.

And once you've developed it? Then it's time to close the sale.

CHAPTER SEVEN

CLOSING ON RELATIVE VALUE

Chapter Seven

RV = BR + RM @ FMP

Closing is all about survival: your customer's personal and professional survival. Survival for the business, user and financial level decision makers.

We described in the last chapter how a Smart Proposal encapsulates those survival needs. It shows how you can address them effectively in a set sequence covering Business Objectives, Alternate Strategies Considered, Solution Overview, Unique Qualifications and Corporate Overview, in that order.

A Smart Proposal presentation is simply a section-by-section direct recital of a Smart Proposal.

Yes, that's exactly what we said. All you have to do is read it out loud.

Walk the stakeholders through it item by item, in their words. State all the reasons described in the proposal driving them to seek a solution, all the reasons alternative solutions are weak, and all the reasons your solution is unique and best fit.

Then stop. And ask for the close.

At this point we know how to use a Smart Fit-Assessment to properly develop your solution and we know how to construct a Smart Proposal that declares Relative Value.

All that's needed at that point is to ask for the close, sign the contract and move forward.

Correctly done, it can literally all be over in minutes.

In fact, it's so simple and compelling that in many cases you can just hand a Smart Proposal to all the participants, read it verbatim, word for word, and close the sale right there, quickly and effectively.

True, it doesn't always happen that easily. There are two schools of thought about closing. One school says that closing is a natural occurrence that follows a good sales process — the assumptive sale. The other school says that closing is an *event*. You have to *ask* for the sale. The sale has to be actively closed.

There's been a long argument between the two approaches. And here's the simple truth: they're both right.

You have to be able to do both. You have to be able to advance the sale by developing a business case so strong that the customer naturally moves forward, all the way through to contract execution. This happens frequently and the stronger your customers are, the more likely it is to happen. This is because the decision-makers you've selected have the courage and internal influence to make the transaction happen. The right decision-makers know how to get deals done internally; they don't need your help to push it through.

But when this doesn't happen, either it's because the customer is not yet fully sold that you're the best fit, or because they don't yet have full buy-in from all members involved in the decision.

Either way, the sale has to be closed and your team has to close it.

There's a moment of truth when a decision needs to be made to buy from you, and that decision has to be able to withstand budget and compliance justification. This is a moment when having a short but formal statement of the strongest reasons why they should buy is valuable: it's the best way to trigger that decision to buy.

This is the perfect time to apply the Relative Value formula:

$$RV = BR + RM@FMP$$

Again, this formula explains Relative Value and states that the relative value of your solution is shown by considering the *business return* (BR) it provides – the increased market share or sales, the reduced work cycle time, improved quality, compliance or profitability – plus the business/purchasing *risk mitigated* (RM) – the aspects of the deal that minimize contractual, performance, reliability and scheduling risks – offered at a *fair market price* (FMP): a price that may not be rock bottom but that is clearly in the commonly accepted range.

A very effective way to close on relative value with a customer is to take out a pencil or marker, write out the formula **RV=BR+RM@FMP**, explain how you arrived there, and – then and there – to ask for the order.

Need an example?

RV=BR+RM@FMP:

"During the Fit-Assessment our teams discovered together that we can achieve a business return by increasing and/or improving _____ and we can do it by fully mitigating the risks associated with _____, _____, _____ and _____.

"This can be done for a total price of _____.

"Would you like to get started?"

It's that simple. And that powerful.

CHAPTER EIGHT

THE INTEGRATION OF MARKETING AND SALES FOR 2017

CHAPTER EIGHT

Everything we've said up to this point in the book works. You've applied it in practice and you are getting real results. It's now 2017. What has to be added in order to capitalize on the natural progression of the B2B technology marketplace?

While the principles of Smart Selling are sound, the media through which you apply them has changed radically. The internet, social media, blogs, texting tools, email and mobile devices – all of these have changed the way businesses and sales people communicate with each other.

Today the buyer is 68% through their evaluation process before they ever talk to a traditional salesperson. They no longer feel the need to engage with, nor do they trust, the traditional salesperson.

Over the past year, how many times have you picked up your smartphone and called a salesperson to learn more about a product or service? Better question: how many times have you made a meaningful purchase because someone cold-called you?

Instead of calling a salesperson for information, you will perform a Google search. You will look at the top websites presented on page one. Within the first five seconds of landing onto a selected site, you will determine if that site teaches you something relevant to the survival of your business. If so, you will go to the About Us tab to see if the people responsible for the organization have the authority to support their claims. From there, you will read or view testimonials from people just like you who achieved the same success that you are looking for. And you will begin to develop a level of trust in the organization.

All without ever talking to a salesperson yet.

As you formulate an opinion of how you can achieve a competitive advantage, you may engage in an online chat with the company thought leaders. You may read, learn and comment on the company blogs, if they are insightful. As you gain more knowledge you may attend a recommended networking function. In almost all cases you will receive an invitation to attend a learning event which you will accept. This could be a webcast, roundtable or seminar. But it won't be a typical product presentation given by a traditional salesperson. It will a learning event on how to improve your organization, provided by a Smart Salesperson.

Eventually you will request more information or ask to get onto the organization's mailing list so you can receive periodic tips, updates and invites. At some point you are invited to connect on LinkedIn, Facebook or Twitter. And at some magical point, you will actually begin following them! You begin to admire the organization. Again, without ever talking to a traditional salesperson.

And at just the right time you will receive an email and a call from a Smart Salesperson, from the organization that you know and admire.

You will learn even more from this conversation. You will be taught about specific benchmarks that can be achieved for your organization. If you feel that the conversation is important or interesting, the Smart Salesperson will suggest deeper discussion to determine your feasibility, potential return and if their offering could be the right fit for you.

That's right, you guessed it: a perfect 5x1.

This is how the best of the best build pipeline. They integrate marketing principles with Smart Sales principles into a cohesive model that creates top of the funnel leads.

So why can't your sales team do this in 2017?

They can. For 2017 we've created a model and sequential guidelines utilizing the Smart Sales Method for generating client interest and converting that interest to top of funnel leads.

You can see a quick overview by reviewing the infographic on the adjacent page. We call it the Lead Generation Organization or LGO. Executing it requires a new integration of B2B marketing and sales. It's not a matter of marketing replacing sales, or vice versa. We integrate marketing and sales because we want to *upgrade* marketing to learn how to sell, and we want to *upgrade* sales teams to perform some key aspects of marketing. The result is that marketing and sales work together in sync to form a Lead Generation Organization or LGO.

Why the emphasis on lead generation? Because lead generation is what generates a robust pipeline, a pipeline that leads to Fit-Assessments, Smart Proposals and ultimately to sales success.

If you think of your web site, your social media site, your entire online presence, all of that now has to be an electronic 5x1. It's all about the idea of sparking the customer's survival instinct, about putting out benchmarks or provocation questions and then converting that to the next logical step – a Fit-Assessment. That's how leads are generated.

So the first step in integrating marketing and sales is to have marketing people understand the 5x1, and to put their 5x1 throughout all of their online media and marketing materials.

Your message is your electronic 5x1, targeted clearly at that business level decision maker, and it's a message that has to be put out consistently throughout your entire print and online media. Especially throughout your entire online presence: your core website, your blogging sites, and your Facebook and LinkedIn pages. It should be vividly present throughout all of your marketing literature, whether you call that literature public relations or a white paper, email or web copy, a one-line tweet or a one-hour webinar script. It has to about the business problem that you solve and the business advantage

THE LEAD GENERATION ORGANIZATION

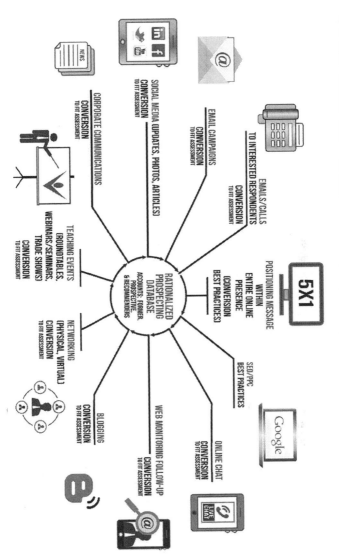

CORPORATE COMMUNICATIONS
CONVERSION TO FIT ASSESSMENT

SOCIAL MEDIA UPDATES, PHOTOS, ARTICLES)
CONVERSION TO FIT ASSESSMENT

EMAIL CAMPAIGNS
CONVERSION TO FIT ASSESSMENT

EMAILS/CALLS TO INTERESTED RESPONDENTS
CONVERSION TO FIT ASSESSMENT

TEACHING EVENTS (ROUNDTABLES, WEBINARS/SEMINARS, TRADE SHOWS)
CONVERSION TO FIT ASSESSMENT

RATIONALIZED PROSPECTING DATABASE
ACCOUNTS: FORMER, PROSPECTIVE, & RECOMMENDERS

POSITIONING MESSAGE WITHIN ENTIRE ONLINE PRESENCE
(CONVERSION BEST PRACTICES)

5X1

SEO/PPC BEST PRACTICES

NETWORKING (PHYSICAL, VIRTUAL)
CONVERSION TO FIT ASSESSMENT

BLOGGING
CONVERSION TO FIT ASSESSMENT

WEB MONITORING FOLLOW-UP
CONVERSION TO FIT ASSESSMENT

ONLINE CHAT
CONVERSION TO FIT ASSESSMENT

you provide.

B2B technology marketing is not to the masses. You are marketing to a tightly segmented niche of decision-makers. The result is much more pinned-down conversations, more predictable content, and involving more one-to-one marketing. The B2B tech salesperson addresses one and only one buyer persona. If you're marketing Coca-Cola, a lot of different people drink Coca-Cola. But if you're marketing tight tolerance polymer optics perfectly aligned to Defense Department applications, you don't have to have wide marketing expertise. All you have to describe is that your lenses are going to achieve target accuracy 100% of the time, and can be produced faster and more cost effectively than their current approach. More safety at a lower cost to the taxpayers.

As discussed in earlier chapters, there are only five drivers in the business-to-business sale. Can what you're offering improve your customer's revenue generation? Can it reduce their cycle time for building a product or delivering a service? Can it improve first time quality? Can it help meet compliance? Does it mean that they make more money or will it save more money?

When you look at the LGO, you see a framework that, step-by-step, allows you to discuss business drivers earlier in their buying cycle. To create an opening for your sales team to make contact at just the right time. And in the new online situation where

68% of prospects are actively searching the web, you want them to find you instead of your competitor. You want your sales team to engage at the right time. And you want to convert to Fit-Assessments and Smart Proposals as soon as possible.

Integrating marketing and sales is the next step for 2017 sales success.

The Positioning Message

Your positioning message is perhaps the most important single element in the lead generation process – and if you've worked through this book from the beginning, you've already completed it. It's nothing more or less than your 5x1.

If you've read through the book and haven't stopped to work out your own 5x1, set some time aside, go back, read the appropriate chapter again, and do so. That message permeates every stage of the lead generation circle you're about to explore. It's not too much to say that all the stages are little more than different ways to convey that statement to your prospective customer.

SEO

SEO refers to search engine optimization and there are only two things that a technology CEO needs to know about SEO.

The first is that you need to have search engine

optimization, and to initiate and use pay-per-click programs. It's no longer a luxury. For small- to medium-sized B2B technology companies, it's a necessity. The only question is whether to outsource it or to dedicate people internally to it.

We strongly recommend that this function be outsourced. Those who disagree are welcome to go to Google and download the 140-plus complex pages detailing their ranking algorithms, or browse the many books discussing Google rankings and their periodic updates. Simply put: it's a matter for professionals. If you assign someone in-house to do it part-time, or even full-time, you'll be beaten in the struggle for page rank, and prospects looking for your services may find your competitors but they won't find you.

There is a bright side of hiring professionals to handle SEO. It allows you to expertly address that part of the lead generation process right out of the box, and focus on the remaining elements all the more quickly and thoroughly.

The second thing is to gain a full appreciation of the Google acronym, "EAT." EAT stands for Expertise, Authority and Trustworthiness. That's how Google ranks and evaluates web pages for quality and search worthiness. Your content doesn't have to be unique. It doesn't have to be novel or radical or brilliantly written. If you're expert, if you're an authority on the topic, and if you're trustworthy, Google will deal with your your pages favorably. Focus on creating quality pages with sound layout – and your SEO consultant will help you there.

Responsibility for search engine optimization, like responsibility for complete and accurate customer data and for a rationalized prospecting database, is a CEO responsibility – the number one CEO responsibility. The CEO needs to make sure that there's an effective web site with a 5x1 and that it's search engine optimized to the best possible degree so that you are found by the right customers.

The salesperson's job is to provoke the client using a 5x1 and to progress to a Fit-Assessment, and a Smart proposal, and convert that prospective customer to a new customer. They will be participating as subject matter experts in live chat conversations, networking organizations, monthly teaching events, presenting at seminars, speaking in online roundtables and webinars, sharing tips and case studies on social media, emailing to interested respondents and picking up the phone and calling people that have expressed an interest. The salesperson needs to focus on selling, meaning on those parts of the Smart Sales methodology he or she is best positioned to execute, and to not waste time on developing expertise in an area much more cost-effectively outsourced.

Live Chat

Once we have a 5x1 embedded within your

online presence, your web site is fully optimized for search engines, and your pay-per-click practices align, you're going to start to see a trickle and then a stream of people coming to your web site.

But what happens then? Do you just hope they read your message and call you? The fact is that only 2% of the people going to your website will call or asked to be contacted. Even if they love your website. You have to increase that number of conversions by using a chat function.

A chat function is a program that lets you communicate directly in real time to visitors of your site. When someone arrives at your website, you're notified that they're there. Your chat option dialogue box opens up on the web page, and the statement "Can I help you?" appears, and you and the visitor engage in a dialogue.

That dialogue is an opportunity to take the visitor *directly into your 5x1*, and convert to a Fit-Assessment and/or Smart Proposal on the spot.

"Thanks for chatting. Can I ask you a few questions? Why is this important or interesting to you? Why now? How do you expect this to impact your business positively? What concerns do you have? What are the ramifications? What solutions have you previously considered?"

Sound familiar?

When a chat function is introduced, you can literally run right through all eleven Fit-Assessment questions in a matter of moments. Not only do you have the opportunity to talk with the customer early in the cycle, you can apply and facilitate all the Smart Sales Methodology principles immediately – the 5x1, the Fit-Assessment, even a Smart Proposal – and bring that inquiry to a sale.

How much does it cost? There are chat functions available for five or ten dollars a month – and less. Some are even free if you allow them to brand the function. There are a variety of chat services available, and installation can be as easy as pressing the install button and configuring it.

A chat function on your site in 2017 is mandatory. But understand the underlying principle. Because it's a principle that permeates every stage of the LGO model. It allows you to electronically extend the Smart Sales Method through all your electronic media. The goal is to reduce the number of stages a lead has to go through in order to contact you directly. And once they do contact you directly, to enable you to go immediately into the 5x1, address their business survival, and move smoothly and quickly into the Fit-Assessment.

Web Traffic Monitoring

Web traffic monitoring is the ability to get a customer's IP address when they come to your website. It's a tool that has the ability to show *who* comes to your website, *what pages* they look at, *how long* they stay on each item, and shows you their IP address and location.

No, it doesn't give you the specific individual, but it does give you the corporate address. Finding the person at that corporate location isn't a problem, because you have a rationalized database as discussed earlier; and if that company is on your targeted list you can easily cross-check to find the business level decision-makers in that company.

At that point you simply call and thank them for their interest and go straight into your 5x1. "We work with companies like yours to significantly improve your business results. Is there something on our site that is important or of interest to you?"

It doesn't have to be a call. You can email them or Skype them or otherwise contact them. But in each case, and whatever the medium, what you're *really* doing is presenting your 5x1 to them and progressing to a Fit-Assessment.

Blogging

Blogging allows you to teach electronically, and that's important for two reasons.

The first is that it helps you establish yourself as a thought leader. If what you have to say is sound, informed, helpful and interesting to your target demographic, you've taken a significant step. As discussed earlier in this book, 77% of the time the customer buys from those they view as the thought leader. Not the brand leader, product leader or the most likable salesperson.

The second reason is that it provides a way for you to convert interested respondents to Fit-Assessments.

Blogs are not a personal publishing service you use because you're in love with the sound of your own voice. And the number of "hits" or "impressions" that you get have little to do with lead generation.

What matters to you are those people who *respond* to your blog post: *those* are the people who have the potential to become customers. Those are the people you can immediately contact back, and say, "Thanks for commenting. Please tell me more about your business objectives and if what we discussed is interesting or important to you. Why? Why now? Why don't we have a meeting, or get together with the right people over a conference call to determine feasibility, potential return, and if we're a good fit?"

Why are *respondents* so important? Because they're sufficiently interested and motivated to *get in touch*. That interested respondent could be someone you met at a networking event, someone who listened to one of your roundtables or attended your seminar, someone who opened up one of your tips or case studies, or someone who gave you a thumbs up or commented on your LinkedIn output or responded to an email you sent.

But that interested person is always the same – *they've* expressed an interest in *you*.

That difference may be subtle, but it's a

difference that makes all the difference in the world to a salesperson. Because it means not having to make an *ice* cold call – the sort of call that is statistically very likely to be rejected. When you contact a respondent, you're not making a cold call at all – you're reaching out to someone who knows your company and knows what it offers and who's expressed an interest and a willingness to communicate. When an opportunity presents itself, all the salesperson has to do is state the 5x1 and do a Fit-Assessment.

What does that salesperson say? Nothing very complicated. At Worldleaders, what we say is, "Thanks for responding to my blog. As you know, we work with CEOs of technology companies to help them improve sales results by up to 100%. Is that something that's important or interesting to you? Really! We should get together."

Yes, what you're deploying is the 5x1, one of the most powerful techniques in the Smart Sales methodology. But in actual practice, it's just something you say in an easy, casual, conversational manner. In fact, virtually everything we've presented in the book up to this point is something you can say to a prospect or potential customer in person or over the phone easily and smoothly, and without any awkwardness or perceived pressure. And a key point of this chapter is that it's not just something you can say in person or over the phone: it's a methodology and a manner you can communicate through the entire range of new digital media.

Networking

Increasingly, the way we interact now is electronically. We learn about each other's company on the web. We see each other's profiles on LinkedIn before we meet in person or call or email one another.

A networking event is nothing more than another interaction in which the salesperson meets a prospective buyer, asks a provocation question or describes a benchmark that would trigger a 5x1, and converts to a Fit-Assessment off-site or on the spot.

But the point of networking is not simply to connect, to chat, to exchange business cards, but to use your 5x1 *with the right person.*

"So what do you do?"

"We work with CEOs of B2B technology companies to improve their sales results by 100%."

"Really? That's interesting."

"Why?"

"To tell you the truth, we'd like our sales to improve."

"We've managed to improve sales up to 100% for companies like yours. Listen, why don't we get together to discuss whether it's feasible to do that for you? We can see if it would be a solid return on investment, and whether we're a good fit."

Instead of just the usual "relationship-building" chitchat about kids and sports, progressing to a 5x1

137

allows you to directly address the survival component that's ever-present and active in the mind of every serious business-level decision-maker.

And you *always* talk first to their survival. Smart salespeople focus constantly on the customer's need to survive in a deeply competitive business environment.

It's important to remember that you are always looking for the *decision-maker*, and *not* for what are sometimes called "influencers." Too often inexperienced or timid sales persons think that making a positive impression on someone associated with or close to a target decision-maker should be cultivated. That's worse than a mistake.

We know from research that people buy from those they perceive to be thought leaders. If you give your message to an influencer, and the influencer does actually bring it up to a decision-maker, they're not going to come across as a thought leader, they're not going to disrupt, they're not going to present your 5x1 properly, they're not going to move to a Fit-Assessment.

There is no reason whatsoever to go to networking events where there are none of your targeted decision-makers present.

Go to networking events where the real decision-makers are, have a real conversation, and you'll get real results.

Teaching Events

Every effective lead generation model includes teaching events. Teaching events are scheduled opportunities to show the prospective client how to improve a business result.

It could be a seminar your organization is holding to which they're invited. It could be a webinar or a webcast. It could be a customer roundtable featuring a customer who's successfully implemented your solution and is taking calls and questions. It could be a talk at a trade show. It could be a conference at which you appear, or one that you organize and run.

But in all these cases you're doing what in *The Challenger Sale* they call "commercial teaching": showing a customer how to improve a business result.

We recommend you hold these events on a monthly basis. They are one of the most effective lead generation events, and in order to get people to come to that event, you have to invite them. And when you do, that in itself is an opportunity to initiate a conversation that flows seamlessly into you presenting your 5x1.

"I'd like to invite you to a seminar about improving sales results for your team."

"What's it about?"

"We will discuss how to grow more pipeline and close more sales. Is that important or interesting to you?"

That gives you an opportunity right then and there to convert to a Fit-Assessment.

So the reality is, you're using the invitation to the event to engineer an opportunity to create pipeline. They don't even have to *go* to the event to do a Fit-Assessment. You may convert them in that very conversation.

That's possible because the invitation itself is a 5x1.

There's a class that we teach on how to run these events. And here's the perfect way to start off: present a benchmark of business objectives that an aspirational company in their industry should be doing.

Then discuss the alternate strategies that a customer can consider – doing nothing, having their internal people or existing partners do it, or looking to external providers.

Then provide a typical solution overview in terms of capability, usability, and reliability.

From there you may say, "If you are going to do something like this, the best way to mitigate risk is to break it down into a schedule that addresses time, contractual risk, performance risk, and reliability risk."

Next, you may talk about how to budget the solution.

Guess what? You've just led a group of high-level decision-makers through a Smart Proposal. And they're on board.

If you revisit the Smart Proposal chapter earlier you will see six proposal components. If you turn them into six easy Powerpoint slides and you did a teaching event on a hypothetical company, you will be spot on.

You will discuss the business objectives that impact strongly on the survival instinct of the decision-makers you've invited. You'll review the alternate strategies they should consider as they reach for those objectives. You'll describe the solution – what it should look like, the pricing terms and conditions that they should look at, and how to evaluate if a firm is uniquely qualified to deliver that solution.

The reality is, if you look at your website, if you look at your online presence, *that's* your teaching event. When you're always teaching you don't have to get ready to teach. When your solution is tied tightly to your market, and your message is tied tightly to market, the calls you make and the things you say are going to be very, very similar. You'll be describing how your product or service will make them money, save them money, help them meet compliance, enable them to deliver their products or solution faster, improve their first time quality – how it will make their business grow, and make them shine in the company's eyes for making a buying decision that makes the company more profitable and more competitive.

Corporate Communications

Corporate communications is a term that is used elsewhere to cover almost any aspect of corporate presentation. But in practice, as we use it here, it involves creating a newsletter that communicates your positioning message to your selected decision-makers.

A good corporate communications newsletter focuses on how to help the customer reading it improve a business result. The structure is generally simple. You want to present material that will show them how to make money, save money, or improve compliance.

So let's say section one opens with the business tip of the month, section two presents one or two relevant industry case studies, section three highlights a new industry development or news item, and section four announces a teaching event. Within all these items we always want to see a business objective being addressed, and we always remember that any testimonials, case studies, product overviews, any social or scheduling event pieces, *everything* should be geared to generate a *response*, a response the sales person can convert into a 5x1 and then into a Fit-Assessment.

Yes, the content of a newsletter should be of interest to its recipient, and it's most likely to achieve that by addressing the reader's business objectives and their survival instinct. But from the Smart Sales standpoint, the whole objective of writing corporate communications such as newsletters is to achieve one goal: we want the reader to *open it.* Mail tracking tools like Constant Contact or Mailchimp can show us who has. And that matters.

Why? Because once a recipient has opened your newsletter, you have an opportunity to connect and move into your 5x1. The *whole focus* of the corporate communication is to see if they've opened your message and to pick up the phone and call them in order to convert to a Fit-Assessment.

Think about it. They've opened up a communication that contains your positioning message, you've delivered it to the right person, the right business-level stakeholder – why not call that person, thank them for reading the newsletter, ask them if they got what they were looking for, and go into your 5x1 and ask if they would like to get together to determine feasibility, return on investment, and best fit?

It's important to emphasize this not only because it's the most effective way to actually move the sales process forward to a successful close, but because so much of so-called marketing efforts do the exact opposite. Barely 1% to 2% of such communications ever get opened because recipients have gotten used to expecting the contents to be more of the same stale talk about why the company that's sending it is the best, the oldest, the greatest, and never about the *recipient's* business objectives.

Time and money is spent on company newsletters no one reads purely because companies are expected to have newsletters, and their use as lead generation tools is ignored.

Remember that everything that we do here – corporate communications, blogs, and social media – is to get a *response* that comes to you. You're not talking to the general public to hear yourself speak. You're putting out a message to the high-level decision-makers in your database in order to get a reaction from them and immediately connect with the decision-maker making that response. You want to get a Like, a Thumbs Up, an Inmail, a Retweet, a *reaction* – so that when you do make a call, it's not a cold call; so that when you connect, they know who you are, they regard you and what your company provides favorably, they buy what you sell, they're pleased that you called.

That's why the subject line of an email newsletter may be more important than its actual content, and an email newsletter is more important than a printed newsletter. It isn't the savings in postage – steep as prices are – it's the fact that we don't know who's read the print version, and we have no opening through which we can connect. Whereas someone who opens an email newsletter, even if they barely glance through it, gives us an opportunity to connect and to *casually,* with a *single sentence,* move into a structured conversation that could then and there conclude with a closed sale.

Social Media

Currently social media is everywhere, and tremendous amounts of employee time and corporate money are being spent on it, with far from impressive returns. The Smart Sales approach to social media operates the same as it does in other stages of the Lead Generation model – in other words, more effectively and more successfully.

We start with focus. In 2017, if you're in B2B technology sales, the most important tool in social media is LinkedIn. Facebook matters to a lesser degree, as does Twitter. But in everything that we do at Worldleaders, we focus is on the highest-probability highest-return selling behaviors and how to integrate them into our day-to-day practices.

In that respect, LinkedIn is by far the single strongest social media leader: if you're a B2B technology salesperson selling technology to the highest-ranking business level decision-makers in your field, you are going to be able to find them and communicate with them far more easily and effectively on LinkedIn than any other media tool.

There are books and courses that go into LinkedIn in great depth, but to deploy Smart Sales approaches on it can involve just a handful of simple – but regular – activities.

If you start off with the Update section on the LinkedIn dashboard, for example, you write a comment or post an image that goes into a general

LinkedIn feed. That item could be a motivational quotation, a notice of an upcoming teaching event, the subject line of an email, even your 5x1. It could be more personal than is usual when business communications are involved. "Went to sales conference. Having a great time." It could be a thank you for a compliment from a reader of your book, or a notice about a story in which you're featured, or your thoughts about the direction of your industry.

The key to them all is the same: you want to put out *provoking* material for people to see and *respond to* by a Thumbs Up, by a request to connect, by an Inmail. You want them to respond to you so that *you* can respond back and convert that into a Fit-Assessment.

Do your due diligence and find information relevant to your market constituency, to your readers. It may be an idea about how they can improve their business. It may be a relevant item of news. It may just be a sentence or two but if it's something they open and respond to, and if you do it one or two times a day, every day, you're going to find that you'll develop an online reputation on LinkedIn, and connect not only with the people in your rationalized database but also with other like-minded individuals.

Remember. Your positioning message should permeate your entire online presence and all your online communications. Does that mean your 5x1 should be an element of your LinkedIn presence? Of course. If you comment on a high-level decision-maker's article and they see you, they should be seeing not a random profile but the profile of a subject matter expert in their field.

When I post to LinkedIn, my signature reads, "Joe Morone - Sales Speaker, Sales Trainer, and Author - www.worldleaderssales.com." That's part of my signature line every time I post or comment. It's a signature – but it's also a message: a positioning message.

There are three kinds of updates we've found to be effective. Posting something early in the day that's humorous, that brightens someone's day, an affirmation, a quotation, a joke – that's using the social side of social media, and it's a welcome message for most readers in the morning. Even in a business setting people will respond to that. One morning I sent out a simple one-line comment: "Friday – only two more work days till Monday." It got a ton of responses. And that's because it was targeted: I knew the kind of people I was sending it to – entrepreneurial CEOs who regard their business as their life, something that accompanies them 24/7.

If the morning revolves around motivation or humor, the afternoon post or comment can be a teaching moment. "Have you considered this?" "Here's a tip I've found helpful." Evening is a good time for some kind of reflection – for accountability. What have you learned today that will enable you to better perform tomorrow? Did you get done what you were supposed to get done today?

Over time the people that connect with become your LinkedIn community. You care about them. You understand their concerns. You understand what drives them.

And because you do, and because you appear regularly, you'll soon find that every day you get responses from people – and not simply people at random, but people in your rationalized database.

And when you see that they've reached out to you, you reach back. "Hey, Bill, it's been a long time, haven't seen you, why don't we get together and chat about how things have been going in the business?" – and about feasibility, and return on investment, and best fit.

Because social media is often a grey area between social interaction and business, it's not even a matter of coming up with something interesting to say all the time, even though there's always some bit of news or some quotation available near at hand. Pictures are eye-catching – and response-generating – too. Motivational pictures with captions are very powerful things to post. Pictures of your business in operation or of you meeting with industry leaders or speaking at a teaching event convey Expertise, Authority and Trustworthiness. Graphics and infographics can condense and convey complex services or processes in one single image. It isn't even a matter of generating any new material at all – commenting on something that a high-level decision-maker in your database has posted can initiate a conversation that can easily turn into a 5x1.

The beauty of digital tools like social media is that they allow you to repurpose material across platforms at little to no cost. Have you written an article that addresses some aspect of your business that matters to your target market? A blog post? Put it on LinkedIn. Include ways for them to respond, and let them know you welcome their response. And when they do? Respond back with a 5x1 and transition into a Fit-Assessment.

A job you've just finished can be a case study, which can double as a press release, which can be material for a blog post, which can be part of a white paper, which can be downloaded from your website – and drive traffic to it. A quotation from any of the above can be used for an afternoon LinkedIn post, serve as a subject line, or be the inspiration for a graphic.

Yes, there are differences between the different stages of implementing your rationalized prospecting database. Social media differs from blogging: blogging is external – it's available to all the world. Social media posting pushes to your social media contacts – who are also for the most part the individuals in your rationalized database.

But both work. Both are worth doing. Both even overlap to such an extent that what works in one can be repurposed to work in the other, at a considerable savings in time and marketing dollars.

But no matter how many forms your material

assumes, they all have the same aim and structure: to communicate your positioning message, and state your 5x1, and to pass from that into a Fit-Assessment.

Email Campaigns

An email campaign is a series of emails aimed to get a customer to want to have a conversation with you about their business objectives and your offerings.

Remember that we are working within your rationalized prospecting database as described earlier.

At this stage of the process the business-level stakeholder receiving your email campaign should be very aware of you and your organization because you included them in your SEO, Chat, Web Traffic Monitoring, Blogging, Teaching Events, Corporate Communications and Social Media. So this campaign is not a cold emailing to a random list or to random people.

When we look at what a good email campaign looks like, all you really have to do is put your 5x1, survival statement or a provocation question in the subject line. If they're interested in improving their competitive business advantage it should get the email open. And if you add your emotional trigger – "Is this important to you? Why? Why now?" – and put that into the body, the movement from that to a response and into a Fit-Assessment is a short step.

In the case of Worldleaders, we send an email with a subject line that says: "Do you feel your sales team is winning big enough and often enough?"

In the body of the email, we say, "We work exclusively with B2B technology CEOs helping their sales team improve sales results up to 100%. Is solving this problem important or interesting to you?"

"If so, let's get together. I plan on calling you tomorrow between the hours of X and Y. If you're not available at that time please respond back with the choice of times and we'll connect then. Thanks."

That is a *perfect* emailed 5x1.

Has it worked? Yes, it has. Do we continue sending if it doesn't get an immediate response? Yes, we do. Sometimes other priorities get in the way of an immediate response. Sometimes other, unknown, factors may interfere with an instant response. We do know that the service we offer can provide a business advantage to that prospect because otherwise they and their company would not be in our database. So we keep the door open, and remain in contact, varying elements in the email slightly.

The first email may ask, "Do you feel your sales team is winning big enough and often enough?" The second could say, "We work with CEOs of technology companies helping them improve sales by 100%." The third one could ask, "Are your sales teams doing what the top-performing sales people do?"

All fundamentally saying the same thing – and

it's always something very much worth saying. It's a slightly different angle each time, and the main changes involve the subject line and the bullet points in the body of the email. Structurally, however, it's the 5x1, pure and simple. We close by suggesting a get-together to determine feasibility, return and whether we are the right fit. And that's the whole email campaign.

Emails/Calls

And now we come to what everyone considers the hardest, scariest, toughest part of the sales process – and what we've made the easiest, the surest, and the most gratifying part of the whole lead generation cycle.

Cold calls and cold emails to complete strangers hurt. They hurt, and sales people avoid them, because calls to complete strangers result in rejection.

But calls and emails to *interested* respondents who have *already* shown a desire to hear from you are an entirely different contact. If you've set up your database properly, if you've worked sequentially through the stages of the lead generation cycle, then the business level stakeholder taking your call is someone who has already found you on Google thanks to your SEO; someone who may have asked you a question on your Live Chat function; someone who reads your blog; someone you may have met at a networking event; someone who may have attended one of your webinars; someone who receives your newsletter, or retweets your tweets, or has connected with you on LinkedIn.

So when *your* call arrives, you're not calling a stranger. You're calling a colleague who knows who you are and what you have to offer, and is *eager* to take that call.

If you took away the positioning message, the optimized web site, the search engine optimization, the blogging, the events, the LinkedIn, if you took all that away, what you would be doing? You'd be calling and emailing someone who's *not* in your database, someone who's *never* heard of you, who *doesn't* know who you are. You may not even have the right *person*, and you're trying to say something to them out of the blue hoping to catch their attention, hoping they're someone who can move the sale forward when they almost certainly are not. Statistically you have a .007% chance of succeeding.

Why in the *world* would you want to do that when you can do it the *smart* way? When you do this step last, *after* all the other phases and stages, instead of putting it first, the way too many sales people feel they have to do, it's no longer an emotional challenge – it's barely a sales function at all. It's a scheduling function. You've met them, you've talked to them, they've read your materials, they're going to your events, they're getting your newsletter, they're commenting on your blog, they're responding to your LinkedIn updates, they're sending you emails and asking you questions. If you were any more in sync with the prospect, you'd be engaged. Why would they *not* want to convert at that point? Why would they *not* want to meet if their interest in you is that constant and that regular?

The fact is, you've established a fan base that looks up to you as a thought leader and wants to hear from you. Why would they not want to hear from you in person at a meeting, and get the benefits of hearing you discuss how they could improve their business results?

What you've done is go from making a call that's riddled with rejection, disruption, confusion, to making a call anyone could make. It takes no talent whatsoever. An administrative assistant could make it.

"Hello. I work for the office of Joe Morone. We understand that you've purchased his book, subscribe to his newsletter, read his LinkedIn updates, and that you've attended his classes and his sales conferences. He'd like to know if you'd be interested in meeting to discuss your sales team's performance."

These few lines are something an intern can read off an index card – and gain a meeting that doesn't so much *make* a sale as puts the *finishing touches* on a lead generation process that has already pre-sold the prospects.

This approach reduces cold calling down to an administrative function – a scheduling function.

And where there's no rejection, there's no avoidance.

Summary

As you read through this book you understand that nothing happens until something is sold. In order for something to be sold we have to be talking to the right customer, creating the right business case, articulating the right proposal, and asking for the close.

The Smart Sales Method addresses these core factors in more depth and with more statistical support than all other approaches in the B2B technology sales field, and so we have 100% confidence that Smart Sales practitioners will continue to dominate their field.

The variable is lead generation. How do you get to the right decision-maker and have a conversation about their business objectives? That is what is changing in the current sales environment. With the right approach in the new electronic environment it's becoming constantly easier and more cost-effective to get the right level decision-maker to come to *you*. More and more prospects are active and knowledgeable buyers who *want* to find a product that gives them a strong business return.

But while the market is there, most sales organizations have not yet caught up with the new realities. Who is responsible for lead generation? Is lead generation a sales function or a marketing function? Is it an inside sales job? Is it the salesperson's job? Is it the account manager's job?

Who is ultimately accountable?

The Lead Generation Organization we present here is an integration of marketing and sales that enables top of funnel lead generation logically and effectively. Marketing, "marcomm," cold calling, warm calling, all those scenarios should simply be called lead generation.

We have no doubt that the focus of tomorrow's strongest and most prosperous B2B technology companies will be integrating marketing and sales so as to develop a lead generation organization – an LGO team – that works together across the eleven functions we've discussed; because lead generation equals all of the activities required to get a qualified business-level buyer interested in a conversation – in *due diligence* – about feasibility, potential return, best fit. That's the work of lead generation.

When you've got good leads, creating the business case and presenting and closing is the easy part. Getting your lead generation organization in place is the first priority. Even before salespeople. Because if you have a good lead generation team, you can do a direct feed to your sales engineers and your sales force. If you can do a direct feed of the good leads to a qualified engineer or CEO, you can close that sale. It will happen. But if you don't have good leads, you have nothing.

Or perhaps we should say: those who have

no idea how to generate good leads have nothing. Because you've just gone through a concise step-by-step blueprint of how to establish a lead generation team that will serve you in 2017. You have a path and a method to the highest degree of success in sales – the Smart Sales Method.

CHAPTER NINE

PUTTING
IT
ALL
TOGETHER

Chapter Nine

By now, you fully appreciate the reasoning: nothing happens until something is sold. You understand that selling has to be the number one priority in your organization. You know that Relative Value (**RV=BR+RM@FMP**) has to be present in every sales conversation. You also know that The Smart Sales Method is the process for putting it all together.

You see how straightforward the Smart Sales Method is. Your team uses the 5x1 to build a strong pipeline. They use the Fit-Assessment to assess the customer's ability to achieve competitive advantage. They use the Smart Proposal to demonstrate Relative Value and close the sale. Your win rates should approach 70%.

You also realize that *every* member of a company sells, and that companies that understand that and practice it are significantly stronger than organizations that simply leave it to the sales department. When the entire company becomes the sales department, and everyone understands that they all have a stake in sales results, that company will outperform their competitors.

We've long predicted a growing integration of marketing and sales, and it's happening. We're seeing more and more marketing people involved in Smart Prospecting at the top of the funnel. We're also seeing more customer service organizations adopt The Smart Sales Method. Who's better positioned to engage in upsell, cross-sell and referral development actions than people supporting a customer day-to-day?

So it's clear that, in years to come, marketing and sales and customer service will become much more integrated, much more effective, and much more powerful.

In this book we've tried to make the concepts of The Smart Sales Method as simple and easy to implement as possible.

We understand that, under pressure, in the field, facing top-level competitors, complicated sales methods don't work. You have to be able to default to a handful of simple but rock-solid effective concepts.

With Smart Sales, it's the Relative Value formula: **RV=BR+RM@FMP**. If we're relentless on that from beginning, middle, to end, it will become our road map.

Smart Sales people are not born: they're made. Almost all sales people come into the profession insufficiently prepared, and almost all of them are trained in what we now know to be the least effective, most out-of-date sales methods. They need to be taught how to open a prospecting conversation with a 5x1, and transition (with the right decision-makers) to a Fit-Assessment, so they can develop complete and accurate business then technical requirements. They need to be coached on how to construct and present a Smart Proposal. And ultimately they need to be able to close on Relative Value when the sale needs to be closed.

Yes, we've done all we can here to provide a clear picture of how this process operates, and to constrain them to just a few simple tools and actions.

Yes, we've significantly reduced the amount of ways to do it wrong, and we've streamlined the ways to do it right.

We've worked to make the book shorter, the process faster, the tools lighter, and the implementation process easier.

We've done what we can to make this book and The Smart Sales Method as clear as possible. Yes, you can implement the entire process by simply applying the concepts of this book and utilizing the tools included.

But if you would like our help, we can work directly with you and your team through portions or the entire implementation. We would be honored to do it.

In most environments a full Smart Sales Method Implementation can be achieved within thirty days. This typically consists of two to three days of our preparation, training and consulting time. For this we apply an anagogical learning model that at first involves group discussion, followed by practice using your actual sales opportunities, and eventually your team will teach back the Smart Sales Method to us.

The intention is that all members of your sales team (marketing, sales, inside sales, sales engineering, account management and customer service) will be able to open a conversation with a 5x1, convert to a Smart Fit-Assessment, construct a Smart Proposal and close on Relative Value. Upon completion each member will receive a certificate of completion.

We unconditionally meant what we said on the back cover of this book and throughout the book. We will be with you every step of the way. Our team is here. We want to get your call, hear your questions, and get your feedback. If you need help implementing the system, we're here to help. If you want to talk to us about the system and learn more about what it can do, we want to talk to you too. Just pick up the phone, send a text or email us.

You deserve to win your fair share!

Joe Morone
www.worldleaderssales.com
LinkedIn.com/in/increasesales
Email: jmorone@worldleaderssales.com
Mobile or text: 585 732-5666

Karen Benjamin
www.worldleaderssales.com
LinkedIn.com/in/worldleaders
Email: kbenjamin@worldleaderssales.com
Mobile or text: 585 399-0651

Marty Smith
www.worldleaderssales.com
LinkedIn.com/in/marty-smith-gm-19814110
Email: msmith@worldleaderssales.com
Mobile or text: 585 399-0653

About The Authors

Joe Morone

CEO and Co-Founder
Worldleaders Inc.

As co-founder and co-owner of Worldleaders Inc., Joe's focus is working with CEO's and Sales leaders assisting them to improve sales results. Specifically this includes sales assessment, sales methodology implementation, sales training and sales management consulting.

He leads Worldleaders' Sales Consulting/Training Practice by working directly with CEO'S and sales teams to implement the right sales strategy, sales methods and sales skills needed to "win their fair share."

Learn more about Joe at LinkedIn at www.linkedin.com/in/increasesales/ or by visiting www.worldleaderssales.com.

He may be reached directly at (585) 732-5666.

Karen Benjamin

Partner, Outsourced Sales Recruiting Practice Leader, and Co-Owner,
Worldleaders Inc.

As co-founder and co-owner of Worldleaders, Karen's passion is working with CEO's and Sales leaders, assisting them to improve sales performance and grow their companies. This includes sales assessment and outsourced sales recruiting.

Karen leads Worldleaders Inc.'s Outsourced Sales Recruiting Practice, a service designed to ensure that Worldleaders clients have a consistent pipeline of top performing sales talent, allowing them to hire the top 25% of all sales performers consistently, objectively, cost-effectively and quickly.

Learn more about Karen at LinkedIn at www.linkedin.com/in/worldleaders/ or by visiting www.worldleaderssales.com.

She may be reached directly at (585) 399-0651.

Marty Smith

General Manager
Worldleaders Inc.

As Worldleaders General Manager, Marty Smith assists in program development and operational leadership. His specialties: 'Best in Class' sales process development and implementation, sales personnel recruiting, organizational sales process assessment, sales personnel training and coaching of sales and operational executives.

Marty is a former business executive in the IT industry. He has crafted numerous successful sales and recruiting strategies for complex technology selling and staffing scenarios, assisting many companies in reaching new levels of sales and profit achievement.

Learn more about Marty by visiting www.worldleaderssales.com.

He may be reached directly at (585) 399-0653.

For Further Information

Go to our website at:

www.worldleaderssales.com

Or call or text our authors, Joe, Marty
or Karen at:

Joe Morone
585-732-5666

Karen Benjamin
585-399-0651

Marty Smith
585-399-0653

HAVE
JOE MORONE
SPEAK

CEO and Co-Founder
Worldleaders Inc.
Author of "The Smart Sales Method 2016"

As co-founder and co-owner of Worldleaders Inc.,
Joe works with CEO's and Sales Leaders, helping
them improve sales results. Specifically this includes
sales assessment, sales methodology implementation,
sales training, and sales management consulting.
He has taught or spoken before hundreds of classes,
trainings, seminars and executive gatherings

Joe leads Worldleaders' Sales Consulting/Training
Practice by working directly with CEO'S and sales
teams to implement the
right sales strategy,
sales methods
and sales skills
needed to help
them "win their
fair share."

Visit Joe at www.linkedin.com/in/increasesales/

OR CALL 585-732-5666